DICTIONARY OF
QUOTATIONS

DICTIONARY OF QUOTATIONS

Bloomsbury Books
London

This edition published 1994 by Bloomsbury Books,
an imprint of The Godfrey Cave Group,
42 Bloomsbury Street, London, WC1B 3QJ.

ISBN 1 85471 550 X

Printed and bound in France
by Maury Eurolivres

Contents

Children & Childhood

Jane Austen
On every formal visit a child ought to be of the party, by way of
provision for discourse.
Sense and Sensibility

Sir J(ames) M(atthew) Barrie
When the first baby laughed for the first time, the laugh broke into a
thousand pieces and they all went skipping about, and that was the
beginning of the fairies.
Peter Pan

Every time a child says "I don't believe in fairies," there is a little
fairy somewhere that falls down dead.
Ibid

Ambrose (Gwinett) Bierce
The fact that boys are allowed to exist at all is evidence of a
remarkable Christian forbearance among men.
San Francisco News Letter 1869

George Gordon (Noel), 6th Lord Byron
A little curly-headed good-for-nothing,
And mischief-making monkey from his birth.
Don Juan

Lewis Carroll [Charles Lutwidge Dodgson]
Child of the pure unclouded brow
And dreaming eyes of wonder!
Through the Looking-Glass and What Alice Found There

Sir Winston (Leonard Spencer) Churchill
There is no finer investment for any community than putting milk
into babies.
Radio broadcast, 1943

R(ichard) H(enry) Dana
Better to be driven out from among men than to be disliked of children.
  The Idle Man: Domestic Life

George Eliot [Mary Ann Evans]
Childhood has no forebodings.
  Mill on the Floss

Thomas Fuller
Children are poor men's riches.
  Gnomologia

(Henry) Graham Greene
There is always one moment in childhood when the door opens and
lets the future in.
  The Power and the Glory

Charles Lamb
Boys are capital fellows in their own way, among their mates; but
they are unwholesome companions for grown people.
  The Old and the New Schoolmaster

Henry Wadsworth Longfellow
Ye are better than all the ballads
That ever were sung or said;
For ye are living poems,
And all the rest are dead.
  Children

A boy's will is the wind's will,
And the thoughts of youth are long, long thoughts.
  My Lost Youth

Sir John Lubbock, 1st Baron Avebury
It is customary, but I think it is a mistake, to speak of happy
childhood. Children are often over-anxious and acutely sensitive.
Man ought to be man and master of his fate; but children are at the
mercy of those around them.
  The Pleasures of Life

John Masefield
He who gives a child a treat
Makes joy-bells ring in Heaven's street,
And he who gives a child a home
Builds palaces in Kingdom come.
  The Everlasting Mercy

John Milton
  The childhood shows the man
As morning shows the day.
  Paradise Regained

Christopher Morley
The greatest poem ever known
Is one all poets have outgrown:
The poetry, innate, untold,
Of being only four years old.
  To a Child

Jean Jacques Rousseau
Lacking all sense of right and wrong, a child can do nothing that is
morally evil, or that merits either punishment or reproof.
  Emile

John Ruskin
Give a little love to a child, and you get a great deal back.
  The Crown of Wild Olive

Antoine de Saint-Exupéry
Grown-ups never understand anything for themselves, and it is
tiresome for children to be always and forever explaining things to
them.
  The Little Prince

Sir Walter Scott
Just at the age 'twixt boy and youth,
When thought is speech, and speech is truth.
  Marmion

William Shakespeare
And then the whining schoolboy, with his satchel
And shining morning face, creeping like snail
Unwillingly to school.
   As You Like It 2

George Bernard Shaw
Youth is a wonderful thing. What a crime to waste it on children.

Muriel Spark
One's prime is elusive. You little girls, when you grow up, must be
on the alert to recognize your prime at whatever time of your life it
may occur.
   The Prime of Miss Jean Brodie

Robert Louis Stevenson
A child should always say what's true,
And speak when he is spoken to,
And behave mannerly at table:
At least as far as he is able.
   A Child's Garden of Verses

Harriet (Elizabeth) Beecher Stowe
"Do you know who made you?"
"Nobody, as I knows on," said the child, with a short laugh…"I
'spect I grow'd. Don't think nobody ever made me."
   Uncle Tom's Cabin

Jonathan Swift
I have been assured by a very knowing American of my
acquaintance in London, that a young healthy child well nursed is at
a year old a most delicious, nourishing, and wholesome food,
whether stewed, roasted, baked, or boiled, and I make no doubt that
it will equally serve in a fricassee, or a ragout.
   *A Modest Proposal for preventing the Children of Ireland from
   being a Burden to their Parents or Country*

William Makepeace Thackeray
When you think that the eyes of your childhood dried at the sight of

a piece of gingerbread, and that a plum-cake was a compensation for the agony of parting with your mamma and sisters; O my friend and brother, you need not be too confident of your own fine feelings.

Vanity Fair

Francis Thompson
Know you what it is to be a child?...It is to believe in love, to believe in loveliness, to believe in belief; it is to be so little that the elves can reach to whisper in your ear; it is to turn pumpkins into coaches, and mice into horses, lownesss into loftiness, and nothing into everything, for each child has its fairy godmother in its own soul.

Shelley

Count Leo (Nikolaevich) Tolstoy
Children are a torment and nothing more.

The Kreutzer Sonata

William Wordsworth
The child is the father of the man.

My Heart Leaps Up

Heaven lies about us in our infancy!
Shades of the prison house begin to close
　　Upon the growing boy.

Intimations of Immortality

Sweet childish days, that were as long
As twenty days are now.

To a Butterfly

Youth & Age

Henry (Brooks) Adams
Young men have a passion for regarding their elders as senile.
The Education of Henry Adams

Henri Frédéric Amiel
To know how to grow old is the masterwork of wisdom, and one of
the most difficult chapters in the great art of living.
Journal, 21 Sept. 1874

Aristophanes
Old men are children for a second time.
Clouds

Guillaume de Salluste, Seigneur du Bartas
Who well lives, long lives: for this age of ours
Should not be numbered by years, days and hours.
Divine Weeks and Works: Fourth Day

Bernard M(annes) Baruch
To me, old age is always fifteen years older than I am.

H(erbert) E(rnest) Bates
An old man looks permanent, as if he had been born an old man.
Death in Spring

John Berryman
I always wanted to be old, I wanted to say
I haven't read that for fifteen years.
His Toy, His Dream, His Rest

The Bible
Rejoice, O young man, in thy youth; and let thy heart cheer thee in
the days of thy youth.
Ecclesiastes 11

When I was a child, I spake as a child, I understood as a child, I thought as a child: but when I became a man, I put away childish things.
1 Corinthians 13

Ambrose (Gwinett) Bierce
Age: that period of life in which we compound for the vices that we still cherish by reviling those that we have no longer the enterprise to commit.
The Devil's Dictionary

Longevity: Uncommon extension of the fear of death.
Ibid

(Robert) Laurence Binyon
They shall grow not old, as we that are left grow old:
Age shall not weary them, nor the years condemn.
Poems for the Fallen

Rupert Chawner Brooke
They love the Good; they worship Truth;
They laugh uproariously in youth;
(And when they get to feeling old,
They up and shoot themselves, I'm told.)
'The Old Vicarage, Grantchester'

Samuel Butler
There's many a good tune played on an old fiddle.
The Way of All Flesh

George Gordon (Noel), 6th Lord Byron
There is an order
Of mortals on the earth, who do become
Old in their youth, and die ere middle age.
Manfred

Years steal
Fire from the mind as vigour from the limb;
And Life's enchanted cup but sparkles near the brim.
Ibid

Lewis Carroll (Charles Lutwidge Dodgson)
"You are old, Father William," the young man said,
  "And your hair has become very white;
And yet you incessantly stand on your head—
  Do you think, at your age, it is right?"
  Alice's Adventures in Wonderland

Sir Winston (Leonard Spencer) Churchill
Twenty to twenty-five! These are the years! Don't be content with
things as they are. "The earth is yours and the fullness thereof."
Enter upon your inheritance, accept your responsibilities.
  Roving Commission: My Early Life

Bejamin Disraeli, 1st Earl of Beaconsfield
Youth is a blunder; manhood a struggle; old age a regret.
  Coningsby

The Youth of a Nation are the Trustees of Posterity.
  Sybil

John Dryden
Men are but children of a larger growth.
  All for Love

George Eliot [Mary Ann Evans]
If youth is the season of hope, it is often so only in the sense that our
elders are hopeful about us.
  Middlemarch

Henri Estienne
Si jeunesse savoit; si viellesse pouvoit.
If only youth had the knowledge; if only age had the strength.
  Les Prémices

Benjamin Franklin
At twenty years of age the will reigns; at thirty the wit; at forty the
judgment.
  Poor Richard's Almanac 1741

All would live long; but none would be old.
  Ibid 1749

Gavarni [Sulplice Guillaume ("Paul") Chevalier]
Les enfants terribles.
The embarassing young.
  Title of a series of prints

Joel Chandler Harris
I am in the prime of senility.
  Attributed, 1906

Seymour Hicks
You will recognize, my boy, the first sign of old age: it is when you
go out into the streets of London and realize for the first time how
young the policemen look.
  They Were Singing by C. Pulling

Washington Irving
Whenever a man's friends begin to compliment him about looking
young, he may be sure that they think he is growing old.
  Bracebridge Hall

Dr Samuel Johnson
Towering in the confidence of twenty-one.
  Boswell's *Life of Johnson*

Charles Kingsley
When all the world is young, lad
And all the trees are green;
  And every goose a swan, lad
  And every lass a queen.
  The Water Babies

Rudyard Kipling
And the measure of our torment is the measure of our youth.
  Gentlemen Rankers

Michel Eyquem de Montaigne
Old age puts more wrinkles in our minds than on our faces.
  Essays

Juan Montalvo

Old age is an island surrounded by death.
  On Beauty

Thomas Moore

What though youth gave love and roses,
Age still leaves us friends and wine.
  National Airs: Spring and Autumn

Benito Mussolini

Youth is a malady of which one becomes cured a little every day.
  On his 50th birthday

Stephen Phillips

A man not old, but mellow, like good wine.
  Ulysses

Alexander Pope

You've play'd and lov'd, and ate and drank, your fill.
Walk sober off, before a sprightlier age
Comes tittering on, and shoves you from the stage.
  Imitations of Horace: Epistles

Saki [Hector Hugh Munro]

The young have aspirations that never come to pass, the old have reminiscences of what never happened.
  Reginald at the Carlton

Seneca

Old age is an incurable disease.
  Epistulae ad Lucilium

William Shakespeare

Your lordship, though not clean past your youth, hath yet some smack of age in you, some relish of the saltiness of time.
  King Henry IV Part II 1

Have you not a moist eye, a dry hand, a yellow cheek, a white beard, an increasing belly? Is not your voice broken, your hand short, your chin double, your wit single, and every part about you blasted with

antiquity, and will you yet call yourself young?
  Ibid

Thou wilt fall backward when thou comest to age
For you and I are past our dancing days.
  Romeo and Juliet 1

Therefore my age is as a lusty winter
Frosty, but kindly.
  As You Like It 2

Then come kiss me, sweet and twenty,
Youth's a stuff will not endure.
  Twelfth Night 2

Crabbed age and youth cannot live together:
Youth is full of pleasance, age is full of care.
  The Passionate Pilgrim

Age, I do abhor thee, youth, I do adore thee.
  Ibid

George Bernard Shaw
Every man over forty is a scoundrel.
  Man and Superman: Maxims for Revolutionists

Youth, which is forgiven everything, forgives itself nothing: age,
which forgives itself anything, is forgiven nothing.
  Ibid

It's all that the young can do for the old, to shock them and keep
them up to date.
  Fanny's First Play

(Lloyd) Logan Pearsall Smith
The denunciation of the young is a necessary part of the hygiene of
older people, and greatly assists the circulation of their blood.
  All Trivia

Sydney Smith
That sign of old age, extolling the past at the expense of the present.
  Lady Holland's *Memoir of the Rev. Sydney Smith*

Sir Richard Steele
There are so few who can grow old with a good grace.
  The Spectator, 1711

Robert Louis Stevenson
Youth is the time to go flashing from one end of the world to the
other both in mind and body; to try the manners of different nations;
to hear the chimes at midnight; to see sunrise in town and country; to
be converted at a revival; to circumnavigate the metaphysics, write
halting verses, run a mile to see a fire, and wait all day long in the
theatre to applaud "Hernani."
  Virginibus Puerisque

Jonathan Swift
No wise man ever wished to be younger.
  Thoughts on Various Subjects, Moral and Diverting

Horace Walpole, 4th Earl of Oxford
Old age is no such uncomfortable thing if one gives oneself up to it
with a good grace, and don't drag it about "to midnight dances and
the public show."
  Letter, 1774

Walt Whitman
Youth, large, lusty, loving—youth full of grace, force, fascination,
Do you know that Old Age may come after you with equal grace,
force, fascination?
  Youth, Day, Old Age and Night

Oscar [Fingall O'Flahertie Wills] Wilde
The old believe everything: the middle-aged suspect everything: the
young know everything.
  Phrases and Philosophies for the Use of the Young Chameleon

Thomas Woodrow Wilson
Generally young men are regarded as radicals. This is a popular
misconception. The most conservative persons I ever met are college
undergraduates.
  Address, 1905

Middle Age

Franklin P. Adams
Years ago we discovered the exact point the dead centre of middle age. It occurs when you are too young to take up golf and too old to rush up to the net.
Nods and Becks

Anonymous
You've reached middle age when all you exercise is caution.

Robert Benchley
A man of forty today has nothing to worry him but falling hair, inability to button the top button, failing vision, shortness of breath, a tendency of the collar to shut off all breathing, trembling of the kidneys to what ever tune the orchestra is playing, and a general sense of giddiness when the matter of rent is brought up. Forty is Life's Golden Age.
In *Bartlett's Unfamiliar Quotations*

Edward Ernest Bowen
Forty years on, growing older and older,
  Shorter in wind, as in memory long,
Feeble of foot, and rheumatic of shoulder,
  What will it help you that once you were strong?
Forty Years On (Harrow School song)

George Gordon (Noel), 6th Lord Byron
Of all the barbarous middle ages, that
  Which is most barbarous is the middle age
Of man; it is—I really scarce know what;
  But when we hover between fool and sage.
Don Juan

Nathaniel Cotton
He who at fifty is a fool
Is far too stubborn grown for school.
Slander

Elmer Davis
When a middle-aged man says in a moment of weariness that he is
half dead, he is telling the truth.
By Elmer Davis, 'On not being Dead, as Reported'

Daniel Defoe
Middle Age is youth without its levity,
And Age without decay.

John Dryden
I am resolved to grow fat, and look young till forty!
Secret Love, or The Maiden Queen

F(rancis) Scott (Key) Fitzgerald
Thirty–the promise of a decade of loneliness, a thinning list of single
men to know, a thinning briefcase of enthusiasm, thinning hair.
The Great Gatsby

It is in the thirties that we want friends. In the forties we know they
won't save us any more than love did.
Notebooks

Johann Wolfgang von Goethe
Once a man's thirty, he's already old,
He is indeed as good as dead.
It's best to kill him right away.
Faust

Bob Hope [Leslie Townes Hope]
Middle age is when your age starts to show around the middle.
Attributed

R(udolph) C(hambers) Lehmann
A boy may still detest age,

But as for me I know
A man has reached his best age
   At forty-two or so.
Middle Age

Don(ald Robert Perry) Marquis
Of middle age the best that can be said is that a middle-aged person
has likely learned how to have a little fun in spite of his troubles.
The Almost Perfect State

Sir Arthur Wing Pinero
From forty till fifty a man is at heart either a stoic or a satyr.
The Second Mrs Tanqueray

Jonathan Swift
I swear she's no chicken; she's on the wrong side of thirty, if she be a
day.
Polite Conversation

Sophie Tucker
Life begins at forty.
Song title

E(lwyn) B(rooks) White
In a man's middle years there is scarcely a part of the body he would
hesitate to turn over to the proper authorities.
The Second Tree from the Corner

Edward Young
   Be wise with speed;
A fool at forty is a fool indeed.
Love of Fame

Death, Dying & Grief

Woody Allen [Allen Stewart Konigsberg]
On the plus side, death is one of the few things that can be done as easily as lying down.
   Getting Even

Death is an acquired trait.
   Woody Allen and His Comedy by E. Lax

Kingsley Amis
Death has got something to be said for it:
There's no need to get out of bed for it.
   'Delivery Guaranteed'

Anaxandrides
It is good to die before one has done anything deserving death.
   Fragment

Francis Bacon
I have often thought upon death, and I find it the least of all evils.
   An Essay on Death

I do not believe that any man fears to be dead, but only the stroke of death.
   Ibid

Honoré de Balzac
What does farewell mean, if not death? But will death itself be a farewell?
   Louis Lambert

Sir J(ames) M(atthew) Barrie
To die will be an awfully big adventure.
   Peter Pan

The Bible

For dust thou art, and unto dust shalt thou return.
   Genesis 3

Death is swallowed up in victory. O death, where is thy sting? O grave, where is thy victory.
   Ibid

And I looked, and behold a pale horse: and his name that sat on him was Death.
   Revelation 6

In the midst of life we are in death.
   The Book of Common Prayer: Burial of the Dead

We therefore commit his body to the ground; earth to earth, ashes to ashes, dust to dust; in sure and certain hope of the Resurrection to eternal life.
   Ibid

Man, that is born of a woman, hath but a short time to live.
   Ibid

John Bright

The Angel of Death has been abroad throughout the land; you may almost hear the beating of his wings.
   House of Commons speech, 1855

Thomas Brown

A leap into the dark.
   Letters from the Dead

Robert Browning

What is he buzzing in my ears?
   "Now that I come to die,
Do I view the world as a vale of tears?"
   Ah, reverend sir, not I!
   Confessions

Robert Burns

O Death! the poor man's dearest friend,

The kindest and the best!
Man was Made to Mourn

Samuel Butler
It costs a lot of money to die comfortably.
Note Books

George Gordon (Noel), 6th Lord Byron
'Tis vain to struggle—let me perish young.
Stanzas to the Po

Old man! 'tis not so difficult to die.
Manfred

Death in the front, Destruction in the rear!
Childe Harold's Pilgrimage

Gaius Julius Caesar
Nothing is easier than to blame the dead.
The Gallic War

Marcus Tullius Cicero
No man can be ignorant that he must die, nor be sure that he may not
this very day.
De Senectute

Dante Alighieri
All hope abandon, ye who enter!
The Divine Comedy: Inferno

Charles Dickens
Grief never mended no broken bones, and as good people's wery
scarce, what I says is, make the most on 'em.
Sketches by Boz: Gin Shops

It is a far, far better thing that I do, than I have ever done; it is a far,
far better rest that I go to, than I have ever known.
A Tale of Two Cities

Benjamin Disraeli, 1st Earl of Beaconsfield
Grief is the agony of an instant; the indulgence of grief the blunder
of a life.
Vivian Grey

Those who have known grief seldom seem sad.
Endymion

John Donne
Any man's death diminishes me, because I am involved in mankind; and therefore never send to know for whom the bell tolls; it tolls for thee.
Devotions upon Emergent Occasions

Ralph Waldo Emerson
Goodbye, proud world! I'm going home;
Thou art not my friend, and I'm not thine.
Poems: Goodbye

Henry Fielding
It hath been often said, that it is not death, but dying which is terrible.
Amelia

Benjamin Franklin
The body of Benjamin Franklin, Printer, (like the cover of an old book, its contents torn out and stripped of its lettering and gilding), lies here, food for worms; but the work shall not be lost, for it will (as he believed) appear once more in a new and more elegant edition, revised and corrected by the Author.
Epitaph on himself, 1728

Thomas Gray
Far from the madding crowd's ignoble strife.
Elegy Written in a Country Churchyard

Horace [Quintus Horatius Flaccus]
Pale Death, with impartial foot, strikes at poor men's hovels and the towers of kings.
Odes

A(lfred) E(dward) Housman
And silence sounds no worse than cheers
After death has stopped the ears.
A Shropshire Lad: To an Athlete Dying Young

The man that runs away
Lives to die another day.
Ibid: The Day of Battle

Aldous (Leonard) Huxley
Death...It's the only thing we haven't succeeded in completely
vulgarizing.
Eyeless in Gaza

Ignore death until the last moment; then when it can't be ignored any
longer have yourself squirted full of morphia and shuffle off in a
coma.
Time Must Have A Stop

Thomas Jefferson
I enjoy good health: I am happy in what is around me, yet I assure
you I am ripe for leaving all this year, this day, this hour.
Letter, 1816

Dr Samuel Johnson
It matters not how a man dies, but how he lives.
Boswell's *Life of Johnson*

Jean de La Bruyère
A long illness between life and death makes death a comfort both to
those who die and to those who remain.
Caractères

Jean de La Fontaine
La mort ne surprend point le sage, Il est toujours prêt à partir.
Death does not surprise the wise man, he is always ready to leave.
Fables: La Mort et le Mourant

George Henry Lewes
The only cure for grief is action.
The Spanish Drama

Georg Christoph Lichtenberg
I am always grieved when a man of real talent dies. The world needs
such men more than Heaven does.
Aphorismen

Henry Wadsworth Longfellow
There is no grief like the grief which does not speak.
  Hyperion

Thomas Babington Macaulay, 1st Baron Macaulay
There are not ten people in the world whose deaths would spoil my
dinner, but there are one or two whose deaths would break my heart.
  Letter to Hannah Macaulay, 1833

Mary Tudor
When I am dead and opened, you shall find "Calais" lying in my heart.
  Holinshed's *Chronicles*

W(illiam) Somerset Maugham
Dying is the most hellishly boresome experience in the world!
Particularly when it entails dying of "natural causes".
  The Two Worlds of Somerset Maugham

Menander
Whom the gods love dies young.
  Moyostikhoi

H(enry) L(ouis) Mencken
Of all escape mechanisms, death is the most efficient.
  A Book of Burlesques

John Milton
Of Man's first disobedience, and the fruit
Of that forbidden tree, whose mortal taste
Brought death into the world, and all our woe.
  Paradise Lost

John Muir
On no subject are our ideas more warped and pitiable than on
death…Let children walk with nature…and they will learn that death
is stingless indeed, and as beautiful as life, and that the grave has no
victory, for it never fights. All is divine harmony.
  A Thousand-Mile Walk to the Gulf

Vladimir Nabokov

Life is a great surprise. I do not see why death should not be an even greater one.

Pale Fire

Dorothy (Rothschild) Parker

How could they tell?

[On being told of the death of President Calvin Coolidge.]

Attributed, 1933

Cesare Pavese

Many men on the point of an edifying death would be furious if they were suddenly restored to life.

Samuel Pepys

I went out to Charing Cross, to see Major-General Harrison hanged, drawn and quartered; which was done there, he looking as cheerful as any man could do in that condition.

Diary, 13 Oct. 1660

Sylvia Plath

Dying
Is an art, like everything else.
I do it exceptionally well.

Lady Lazarus

Alexander Pope

But thousands die, without or this or that,
Die, and endow a college or a cat.

Moral Essays

Marcel Proust

Happiness is beneficial for the body, but it is grief that develops the powers of the mind.

Remembrance of Things Past

Jean Jacques Rousseau

All men are afraid of dying, this is the great law of sentient beings, without which the entire human species would soon be destroyed.

Julie, or the New Eloise

Nicholas Rowe
Death is the privilege of human nature,
And life without it were not worth our taking.
  The Fair Penitent

Saki [Hector Hugh Munro]
Waldo is one of those people who would be enormously improved
by death.
  Beasts and Super-Beasts: The Feast of Nemesis

Alan Seeger
I have a rendezvous with Death
At some disputed barricade,
At midnight in some flaming town.
  I Have a Rendezvous with Death

William Shakespeare
A man can die but once.
  King Henry IV, Part II 3

Set honour in one eye and death i' the other,
And I will look on both indifferently.
  Julius Caesar 1

When beggars die, there are no comets seen;
The heavens themselves blaze forth the death of princes.
  Ibid 2

Cowards die many times before their deaths;
The valiant never taste of death but once.
  Ibid

Why, he that cuts off twenty years of life
Cuts off so many years of fearing death.
  Ibid 3

To be or not to be: that is the question:
Whether 'tis nobler in the mind to suffer
The slings and arrows of outrageous fortune,
Or to take arms against a sea of troubles,
And by opposing end them? To die: to sleep.
  Hamlet 3

If I must die
I will encounter darkness as a bride,
And hug it in mine arms.
  Measure for Measure 3

Nothing in his life
Became him like the leaving it; he died
As one that had been studied in his death
To throw away the dearest thing he ow'd,
As 'twere a careless trifle.
  Macbeth 1

Tomorrow, and tomorrow, and tomorrow,
Creeps in this petty pace from day to day,
To the last syllable of recorded time;
And all our yesterdays have lighted fools
The way to dusty death. Out, out, brief candle!
  Macbeth 5

The stroke of death is as a lover's pinch
Which hurts, and is desired.
  Antony and Cleopatra 5

He that dies pays all debts.
  The Tempest 3

"Stevie" (Florence Margaret) Smith
I was much too far out all my life
And not waving but drowning.
  Not Waving but Drowning

Edmund Spenser
Sleep after toil, port after stormy seas,
Ease after war, death after life, does greatly please.
  The Faerie Queene

Stanislaus Leszczynski
He who fears death dies every time he thinks of it.
  Oeuvres du philosophe bienfaisant

Robert Louis Stevenson
Under the wide and starry sky,
Dig the grave and let me lie.
  Requiem

Suetonius [Gaius Suetonius Tranquillus]
Ave, Imperator, morituri te salutant.
Hail, Caesar, those about to die salute thee.
  Life of Claudius

Jonathan Swift
I shall be like that tree, I shall die at the top.
  Memoirs of Jonathan Swift by Sir Walter Scott

Alfred, Lord Tennyson
Half a league, half a league,
  Half a league onward,
All in the valley of Death
Rode the six hundred.
  The Charge of the Light Brigade

Their's not to make reply,
Their's not to reason why,
Their's but to do and die:
  Ibid

Dylan Thomas
Do not go gentle into that good night,
Old age should burn and rave at close of day;
Rage, rage against the dying of the light.
  Do Not Go Gentle

Mark Twain [Samuel Langhorne Clemens]
All say, "How hard it is that we have to die"—a strange complaint to
come from the mouths of people who have had to live.
  Pudd'nhead Wilson

The reports of my death are greatly exaggerated.
  Cable to Associated Press from Europe

John Webster

I saw him now going the way of all flesh.
Westward Hoe

Death hath ten thousand several doors
For men to take their exit.
The Duchess of Malfi

Oscar (Fingall O'Flahertie Wills) Wilde

A thing is not necessarily true because a man dies for it.
Sebastian Melmoth

One can survive anything nowadays except death.
A Woman of No Importance

William Wordsworth

There is
One great society alone on earth;
The noble Living and the noble Dead.
The Prelude

Last Words

Joseph Addison
I have sent for you that you may see how a Christian can die.

Alexander the Great
I die by the help of too many physicians.

Henry Ward Beecher
Now comes the mystery.

Ludwig van Beethoven
I shall hear in heaven.

Anne Boleyn
The executioner is, I believe, very expert, and my neck is very slender.

James Drummond Burns
I have been dying for twenty years, now I am going to live.

Elizabeth I
All my possessions for a moment of time.

Gaius Julius Caesar
Et tu, Brute!
You too, Brutus!

Charles II
Don't let poor Nelly starve. [His mistress, Nell Gwynne.]

He had been, he said, a most unconscionable time dying, but he hoped that they would excuse it.
   Macauley's *History of England*

Oliver Cromwell
It is not my design to drink or to sleep, but my design to make what haste I can to be gone.

Georges Jacques Danton
Be sure you show my head to the mob. It will be a long time ere they see its like.
At his execution

George Eastman
My work is done. Why wait?
His suicide note

Kathleen Ferrier
Now I'll have *eine kleine* pause.

Charles James Fox
I die happy.

George IV
Wally, what is this? It is death, my boy: they have deceived me.
To his page, Sir Walthen Waller

St Gregory VII
I have loved justice and hated iniquity: therefore I die in exile.

Henry VIII
All is lost. Monks, monks, monks!

O. Henry [William Sydney Porter]
Turn up the lights—I don't want to go home in the dark.
Quoting a popular song by Harry H. Williams

Thomas Hobbes
I am about to take my last voyage, a great leap in the dark.

"Stonewall" (Thomas Jonathan) Jackson
Let us cross the river, and rest under the trees.

John Keats
I feel the flowers growing over me.

Cotton Mather
Is this dying? Is this all? Is this what I feared when I prayed against a hard death? Oh, I can bear this! I can bear it!

Sir Thomas More
I pray you, I pray you, Mr Lieutenant, see me up safe, and for my coming down let me shift for myself.
At his execution

Henry John Temple, 3rd Viscount Palmerston
Die, my dear doctor, that's the last thing I shall do!
Attributed

Anna Pavlova
Get my Swan costume ready.

William Pitt the Younger
I think I could eat one of Bellamy's veal pies.

Sir Walter Raleigh
So the heart be right, it is no matter which way the head lieth.
At his execution

Theodore Roosevelt
Put out the light.

Henry David Thoreau
I leave this world without a regret.

Sir Henry Vane
Death is but a little word, but 'tis a great work to die.
On the scaffold

Voltaire [François Marie Arouet]
Do let me die in peace.

Oscar (Fingall O'Flahertie Wills) Wilde
I expect I shall have to die beyond my means.
Taking a glass of champagne on his deathbed

Happiness & Sorrow

Aeschylus
Who, save the gods, can be happy all life long?
  Agamemnon

Jane Austen
Perfect happiness, even in memory, is not common.
  Emma

William Blake
The busy bee has no time for sorrow.
  The Marriage of Heaven and Hell: Proverbs of Hell

Ancius Manlius Severinus Boethius
Nothing is miserable unless you think it so; conversely, every lot is
happy if you are content with it.
  Consolationis Philosophiæ

Sir Thomas Browne
To enjoy true happiness we must travel into a very far country, and
even out of ourselves.
  Christian Morals

Robert Browning
Make us happy and you make us good.
  The Ring and the Book

George Gordon (Noel), 6th Lord Byron
  There comes
For ever something between us and what
We deem our happiness.
  Sardanapalus

Charles Caleb Colton
He that thinks himself the happiest man, really is so.
  Lacon

Dante Alighieri
Nessun maggior dolore,
Che ricordarsi del tempo felice
Nella miseria.
No greater sorrow than to recall in our misery the time when we were happy.
  The Divine Comedy: Inferno

Ralph Waldo Emerson
To fill the hour—that is happiness.
  Essays, First Series: Experience

Edward FitzGerald
Here with a Loaf of Bread beneath the Bough,
A Flask of Wine, a Book of Verse—and Thou
Beside me singing in the Wilderness—
And Wilderness is Paradise enow.
  The Rubaiyat of Omar Khayyam

Thomas Fuller
When sorrow is asleep, wake it not.
  Gnomologia

Théophile Gautier
Happiness is white and pink.
  Caprices et zigzags

Robert B(rowning) Hamilton
I walked a mile with Sorrow
  And ne'er a word said she;
But, oh, the things I learned from her
  When Sorrow walked with me.
  Along the Road

Nathaniel Hawthorne
Happiness in this world, when it comes, comes incidentally. Make it the object of pursuit, and it leads us a wild-goose chase, and is never attained. Follow some other object, and very possibly we may find

that we have caught happiness without dreaming of it.
   American Notebooks

William Hazlitt
I have wanted only one thing to keep me happy, but wanting that
have wanted everything.
   Winterslow: My First Acquaintance with Poets

Thomas Hood
So sorrow is shared by being poured
From one vessel into another.
   Miss Kilmansegg: Her Misery

"Kin" (Frank McKinney) Hubbard
It's pretty hard to tell what does bring happiness; poverty and wealth
have both failed.
   Abe Martin's Broadcast

Victor Hugo
The misery of a child is interesting to a mother, the misery of a
young man is interesting to a young woman, the misery of an old
man is interesting to nobody.
   Les Misérables

Aldous (Leonard) Huxley
Happiness is like coke—something you get as a by-product in the
process of making something else.
   Point Counter Point

Thomas Jefferson
He is happiest of whom the world says least, good or bad.
   Letter to John Adams, 1786

François, Duc de La Rochefoucauld
We are more interested in making others believe we are happy than
in trying to be happy ourselves.
   Maxims

The happiness or unhappiness of men depends no less upon their
dispositions than on their fortunes.
   Ibid

We are never so happy, nor so unhappy, as we think we are.
Ibid

Henry Wadsworth Longfellow
Believe me, every man has his secret sorrows, which the world knows not; and oftentimes we call a man cold when he is only sad.
Hyperion

Into each life some rain must fall,
Some days must be dark and dreary.
The Rainy Day

John Stuart Mill
Ask yourself whether you are happy, and you cease to be so.
Autobiography

Unquestionably, it is possible to do without happiness; it is done involuntarily by nineteen-twentieths of mankind.
Utilitarianism

Molière [Jean-Baptiste Poquelin]
Unbroken happiness is a bore: it should have ups and downs.
Les fourberies de Scapin

Lady Mary Wortley Montagu
One would suffer a great deal to be happy.
Letter, 1759

Thomas Moore
Earth has no sorrow that Heaven cannot heal.
Come, Ye Disconsolate

Alexander Pope
O happiness! our being's end and aim!
Essay on Man

John Ray
Little children, little sorrows; big children, big sorrows.
English Proverbs

Bertrand (Arthur William) Russell, 3rd Earl Russell
The secret of happiness is this: let your interests be as wide as

possible, and let your reactions to the things and persons that interest you be as far as possible friendly rather than hostile.
   The Conquest of Happiness

Men who are unhappy, like men who sleep badly, are always proud of the fact.
   In *The Faber Book of Aphorisms*

Thomas Shadwell
No man is happy but by comparison.
   The Virtuoso

William Shakespeare
Sorrow breaks seasons and reposing hours,
Makes the night morning, and the noon-tide night.
   Richard III 1

More in sorrow than in anger.
   Hamlet 1

When sorrows come, they come not single spies,
But in battalions!
   Ibid 4

All's cheerless, dark, and deadly.
   King Lear 5

Sorrow concealed, like an oven stopp'd,
Doth burn the heart to cinders where it is.
   Titus Adronicus 3

George Bernard Shaw
We have no more right to consume happiness without producing it than to consume wealth without producing it.
   Candida

A lifetime of happiness! No man alive could bear it: it would be hell on earth.
   Man and Superman

Richard Brinsley Sheridan
'Tis now six months since Lady Teazle made me the happiest of

men—and I've been the most miserable dog ever since.
   The School for Scandal

(Lloyd) Logan Pearsall Smith
There are few sorrows, however poignant, in which a good income is
of no avail.
   Afterthoughts

C(harles) H(addon) Spurgeon
Sorrows are visitors that come without invitation.
   John Ploughman

Robert Louis Stevenson
There is no duty we so much underrate as the duty of being happy.
   Virginibus Puerisque

Publilius Syrus
No man is happy unless he believes he is.
   Sententiae

Horace Walpole, 4th Earl of Oxford
The world is a comedy to those that think, a tragedy to those that
feel.
   Letter, 1776

Oscar (Fingall O'Flahertie Wills) Wilde
Where there is sorrow, there is holy ground.
   De Profundis

Money, Wealth & Poverty

John Quincy Adams
The extremes of opulence and want are more remarkable, and more constantly obvious, in this country than in any other that I ever saw.
  Diary

Abbé Leonor Jean d'Allainval
L'embarrases des richesses.
The embarrassment of riches.
  Title of a play

Aristotle
Men are divided between those who are as thrifty as if they would live forever, and those who are as extravagant as if they were going to die the next day.
  Lives and Opinions of Eminent Philosophers by Diogenes Laertius

Francis Bacon
And money is like muck, not good except it be spread.
  Essays: Of Seditions and Troubles

Riches are for spending.
  Essays: Of Expense

Walter Bagehot
Poverty is an anomaly to rich people. It is very difficult to make out why people who want dinner do not ring the bell.
  Literary Studies

Maurice Baring
If you would know what the Lord God thinks of money, you have only to look at those to whom he gives it.
  Writers at Work by Dorothy Parker

Brendan Behan
Pound notes is the best religion in the world.
  The Hostage

Aphra Behn
Money speaks sense in a language all nations understand.
 The Rover

(Joseph) Hilaire (Pierre) Belloc
I'm tired of Love: I'm still more tired of Rhyme.
But Money gives me pleasure all the time.
 Epigrams: Fatigue

The Bible
A good name is rather to be chosen than great riches, and loving favour rather than silver and gold.
 Proverbs 22

No man can serve two masters…Ye cannot serve God and mammon.
 Matthew 6

It is easier for a camel to go through the eye of a needle, than for a rich man to enter into the kingdom of God.
 Ibid 19

For the love of money is the root of all evil.
 1 Timothy 6

Henry St John, Viscount Bolingbroke
All our wants, beyond those which a very moderate income will supply, are purely imaginary.
 Letter to Jonathan Swift, 1719

Samuel Butler
It has been said that the love of money is the root of all evil. The want of money is so quite as truly.
 Erewhon

George Gordon (Noel), 6th Lord Byron
Ready money is Aladdin's lamp.
 Don Juan

Thomas Carlyle
Aristocracy of the money bag.
 History of the French Revolution

Cash payment is not the sole nexus of man with man.
Past and Present

Miguel de Cervantes (Saavedra)
That which costs little is less valued.
Don Quixote

There are but two families in the world as my grandmother used to say, the Haves and the Have-nots.
Ibid

Philip Dormer Stanhope, 4th Earl of Chesterfield
I knew once a very covetous, sordid fellow, who used to say, "Take care of the pence, for the pounds will take care of themselves."
Letters to His Son

Sir Winston (Leonard Spencer) Churchill
Saving is a very fine thing. Especially when your parents have done it for you.
Attributed

William Cobbett
To be poor and independent is very nearly an impossibility.
Advice to Young Men

Charles Dickens
Annual income twenty pounds, annual expenditure nineteen nineteen six, result happiness. Annual income twenty pounds, annual expenditure twenty pounds ought and six, result misery.
David Copperfield

Benjamin Disraeli, 1st Earl of Beaconsfield
"Two nations; between whom there is no intercourse and no sympathy"..."You speak of—" said Egremont, hesitatingly. "The rich and the poor."
Sybil

Ralph Waldo Emerson
Can anybody remember when the times were not hard and money not scarce?
Society and Solitude: Works and Days

George Farquhar
My Lady Bountiful.
   The Beaux' Stratagem

'Tis still my maxim, that there is no scandal like rags, nor any crime so shameful as poverty.
   Ibid

Henry Fielding
Money will say more in one moment than the most eloquent lover can in years.
   The Miser

Benjamin Franklin
Nothing but money is sweeter than honey.
   Poor Richard's Almanack 1735

Many a man would have been worse if his estate had been better.
   Ibid 1751

J(ean) Paul Getty
If you can actually count your money then you are not really a rich man.
   The Pendulum Years by Bernard Levin

Gracchus [François Noël Babeuf]
Let the revolting distinction of rich and poor disappear once and for all.
   Manifesto of the Equals

E(dgar) W(atson) Howe
A man is usually more careful of his money than he is of his principles.
   Ventures in Common Sense

Dr Samuel Johnson
There are few ways in which a man can be more innocently employed than in getting money.
   Boswell's *Life of Johnson*

No man but a blockhead ever wrote except for money.
   Ibid

It is better to live rich than to die rich.
   Ibid

D(avid) H(erbert) Lawrence

Money is our madness, our vast collective madness.

Money Madness

Edward Moore

I am rich beyond the dreams of avarice.

The Gamester

Thomas Love Peacock

Respectable means rich, and decent means poor. I should die if I heard my family called decent.

Crotchet Castle

Titus Maccius Plautus

You must spend money, if you wish to make money.

Asinaria

Jean Jacques Rousseau

Money is the seed of money, and the first guinea is sometimes more difficult to acquire than the second million.

Discours sur l'origine de l'inegalité

William Shakespeare

Saint-seducing gold.

Romeo and Juliet 1

Bell, book, and candle shall not drive me back,
When gold and silver becks me to come on.

King John 3

Neither a borrower nor a lender be.

Hamlet 1

Percy Bysshe Shelley

Wealth is a power usurped by the few, to compel the many to labour for their benefit.

Queen Mab, Notes

Adam Smith

No society can surely be flourishing and happy, of which the far

greater part of the members are poor and miserable.
The Wealth of Nations

(Lloyd) Logan Pearsall Smith
The wretchedness of being rich is that you live with rich people.
Afterthoughts

William Somerville
Let all the learned say what they can,
'Tis ready money makes the man.
Ready Money

Henry David Thoreau
That man is the richest whose pleasures are the cheapest.
Journal, 11 March 1856

Mark Twain [Samuel Langhorne Clemens]
Few of us can stand prosperity. Another man's, I mean.
Pudd'nhead Wilson

Artemus Ward [Charles Farrar Browne]
Let us all be happy and live within our means, even if we have to
borrow the money to do it with.
Natural History

H(erbert) G(eorge) Wells
I don't 'old with Wealth. What is Wealth? Labour robbed out of the
poor.
Autocracy of Mr Parham

Success, Fame & Greatness

Woody Allen [Allen Stewart Konigsberg]
I don't want to achieve immortality through my work. I want to achieve it through not dying.
   Woody Allen and His Comedy by E. Lax

John Emerich Edward Dalberg, 1st Baron Acton
Great men are almost always bad men…There is no worse heresy than that the office sanctifies the holder of it.
   Letter to Bishop Creighton, 1887

Fred Allen [John Florence Sullivan]
A celebrity is a person who works hard all his life to become known, then wears dark glasses to avoid being recognized.
   Treadmill to Oblivion

Henri Frédéric Amiel
Great men are the real men: in them nature has succeeded.
   Journal, 13 Aug. 1865

Francis Bacon
Men in great places are thrice servants: servants of the Sovereign or State; servants of Fame; and servants of Business…It is a strange desire to seek Power and to lose Liberty.
   Essays: Of Great Place

The Bible
Let us now praise famous men.
   Ecclesiasticus 44

Elizabeth Barrett Browning
   A great man,
Leaves clean work behind him, and requires
No sweeper up of the chips.
   Aurora Leigh

Edward (George Earle Lytton) Bulwer-Lytton, 1st Baron Lytton
Beneath the rule of men entirely great,
The pen is mightier than the sword.
 Richelieu

Edmund Burke
It is the nature of all greatness not to be exact.
 Speech, 1774

Passion for fame; a passion which is the instinct of all great souls.
 Ibid

George Gordon (Noel), 6th Lord Byron
I awoke one morning and found myself famous.
 [On the success of *Childe Harold*.]

 Pedro Calderón de la Barca

Fame, like water, bears up the lighter things, and lets the weighty sink.
 Adventures of Five Hours

Dante Alighieri
Chè, seggendo in piuma,
In fama non si vien, nè sotto coltre.
For fame is not won by lying on a feather bed nor under a canopy.
 Divine Comedy: Inferno

John Dryden
His grandeur he derived from Heaven alone,
For he was great, ere fortune made him so.
 Heroic Stanzas after Cromwell's Funeral

Ralph Waldo Emerson
The great man is he who in the midst of the crowd keeps with perfect
sweetness the independence of solitude.
 Essays, First Series: Self-Reliance

To be great is to be misunderstood.
 Ibid

Henry Fielding
Greatness consists in bringing all manner of mischief on mankind,

and goodness in removing it from them.
Jonathan Wild the Great

Benjamin Franklin

I pronounce it as certain that there was never yet a truly great man that was not at the same time truly virtuous.
The Busy-Body

Thomas Fuller

The great and the little have need of one another.
Gnomologia: Adagies and Proverbs

Henry IV

Great eaters and great sleepers are incapable of doing anything that is great.
Attributed

George Herbert

The great would have none great, and the little all little.
Jacula Prudentum

There would be no great ones if there were no little ones.
Ibid

John Keats

Fame, like a wayward girl, will still be coy
To those who woo her with too slavish knees.
Sonnet: On Fame

Jean de La Bruyère

The nearer we come to great men the more clearly we see they are only men. They rarely seem great to their valets.
Caractères

Henry Wadsworth Longfellow

Lives of great men all remind us
  We can make our lives sublime,
And, departing, leave behind us
  Footprints on the sands of time.
A Psalm of Life

The heights by great men reached and kept
  Were not attained by sudden flight,
But they, while their companions slept,
  Were toiling upward in the night.
    The Ladder of Saint Augustine

Alexander Pope
Nor fame I slight, nor for her favours call;
She comes unlook'd for, if she comes at all.
    The Temple of Fame

William Shakespeare
Be not afraid of greatness: some are born great, some achieve
greatness, and some have greatness thrust upon them.
    Twelfth Night 2

George Bernard Shaw
If a great man could make us understand him we should hang him.
    Man and Superman: Maxims for Revolutionists

Life levels all men: death reveals the eminent.
    Ibid

Percy Bysshe Shelley
Fame is love disguised.
    Epipsychidion

Horace Walpole, 4th Earl of Oxford
They who cannot perform great things themselves may yet have a
satisfaction in doing justice to those who can.
    Attributed

John Wolcot ["Peter Pindar"]
What rage for fame attends both great and small!
Better be d——d than mentioned not at all!
    More Lyric Odes to the Royal Academicians

Beauty

Anacreon
Beauty is proof against spears and shields. She who is beautiful is more formidable than fire and iron.
   Fragment

Francis Bacon
There is no Excellent Beauty, that hath not some strangeness in the proportion.
   Essays: Of Beauty

Aphra Behn
Do you not daily see fine clothes…are more inviting than Beauty unadorn'd?
   The Rover

Robert Browning
If you get simple beauty, and nought else.
You get about the best thing God invents.
   Fra Lippo Lippi

Edmund Burke
I never remember that anything beautiful…was ever shown, though it were to a hundred people, that they did not all immediately agree that it was beautiful.
   The Sublime and Beautiful

George Gordon (Noel), 6th Lord Byron
She walks in beauty like the night
   Of cloudless climes and starry skies;
And all that's best of dark and bright
   Meet in her aspect and her eyes:
   She Walks in Beauty

Luis Cernuda
Everything beautiful has its moment and then passes away.
  Las Ruinas

Confucius
Everything has its beauty but not everyone sees it.
  Analects

William Congreve
There is in true beauty, as in courage, somewhat which narrow souls
cannot dare to admire.
  The Old Bachelor

John Donne
No spring nor summer beauty hath such grace
As I have seen in one autumnal face.
  Elegies: The Autumnal

Henry Havelock Ellis
Beauty is the child of love.
  Impressions and Comments

Ralph Waldo Emerson
Beauty is its own excuse for being.
  The Rhodora

Anne Frank
Think of all the beauty still left around you and be happy.
  The Diary of a Young Girl

Baltasar Gracián
Beauty and folly are generally companions.
  The Art of Wordly Wisdom

John Keats
A thing of beauty is a joy forever;
Its loveliness increases; it will never
Pass into nothingness.
  Endymion

"Beauty is truth, truth beauty,"—that is all
Ye know on earth, and all ye need to know.
   Ode on a Grecian Urn

Christopher Marlowe
Was this the face that launch'd a thousand ships
And burnt the topless towers of Ilium? [Of Helen of Troy.]
   Dr Faustus

O, thou art fairer than the evening air
Clad in the beauty of a thousand stars.
   Ibid

John Milton
Beauty is nature's coin, must not be hoarded,
But must be current.
   Comus

Beauty stands
In the admiration only of weak minds
Led captive.
   Paradise Regained

Molière [Jean-Baptiste Poquelin]
Beauty of face is a frail ornament, a passing flower, a momentary
brightness belonging only to the skin.
   Les Femmes savantes

Plato
The good is the beautiful.
   Lysis

Alexander Pope
Beauties in vain their pretty eyes may roll...but merit wins the soul.
   The Rape of the Lock

John Ruskin
Remember that the most beautiful things in the world are the most
useless.
   The Stones of Venice

William Shakespeare
Is she kind as she is fair?
For beauty lives with kindness.
The Two Gentlemen of Verona 4

He hath a daily beauty in his life
That makes me ugly.
Othello 5

Shall I compare thee to a summer's day?
Thou art more lovely and more temperate:
Rough winds do shake the darling buds of May,
And summer's lease hath all too short a date.
Sonnets 18

James Thomson
Perfecty beauty is its own sole end.
Weddah

Count Leo (Nikolaevich) Tolstoy
It is amazing how complete is the delusion that beauty is goodness.
The Kreutzer Sonata

Lew(is) Wallace
Beauty is altogether in the eye of the beholder.
The Prince of India

Oscar (Fingall O'Flahertie Wills) Wilde
Beauty is the only thing that time cannot harm. Philosophies fall
away like sand, and creeds follow one another like the withered
leaves of autumn; but what is beautiful is a joy for all seasons and a
possession for all eternity.
The English Renaissance of Art

It is better to be beautiful than to be good. But…it is better to be
good than to be ugly.
The Picture of Dorian Gray

Nature

Alfonso the Wise [Alfonso X]
Had I been present at the Creation, I would have given some useful hints for the better ordering of the universe.
   Attributed

St Augustine of Hippo
All nature is good.
   Of Continence

Walter Bagehot
Taken as a whole, the universe is absurd.
   Literary Studies

George Gordon (Noel), 6th Lord Byron
There is a pleasure in the pathless woods,
There is a rapture on the lonely shore,
There is society, where none intrudes,
By the deep sea and music in its roar:
I love not man the less, but Nature more…
To mingle with the Universe, and feel
What I can ne'er express, yet cannot all conceal.
   Childe Harold's Pilgrimage

Marcus Tullius Cicero
Those things are better which are perfected by nature than those which are finished by art.
   De Natura Deorum

Ralph Waldo Emerson
Nature is an endless combination and repetition of very few laws. She hums the old well-known air through innumerable variations.
   History

Enrico Fermi
Whatever Nature has in store for mankind, unpleasant as it may be, men must accept, for ignorance is never better than knowledge.
Atoms in the Family by Laura Fermi

Robert (Lee) Frost
How many times it thundered before Franklin took the hint! How many apples feel on Newton's head before he took the hint! Nature is always hinting at us. It hints over and over again. And suddenly we take the hint.

Horace [Quintus Horatius Flaccus]
Though you drive away Nature with a pitchfork she always returns.
Epistles

Thomas Henry Huxley
For every man the world is as fresh as it was at the first day, and as full of untold novelties for him who has the eyes to see them.
A Liberal Education

William Ralph Inge
The whole of nature is a conjugation of the verb to eat, in the active and the passive.
Outspoken Essays

Juvenal [Decimus Junius Juvenalis]
Never does nature say one thing and wisdom another.
Satires

Baron Gottfried Wilhelm von Leibnitz
In nature there can never be two beings that are exactly alike.
The Monadology

Leonardo da Vinci
Nature never breaks her own laws.
Notebooks

Carolus Linnaeus [Carl von Linné]
Nature does not proceed by leaps.
Philosophia Botanica

John Muir
The clearest way into the Universe is through a forest wilderness.
John of the Mountains

Cardinal John Henry Newman
Living Nature, not dull Art
Shall plan my ways and rule my heart.
Nature and Art

Alexander Smith
Nature never quite goes along with us. She is sombre at weddings, sunny at funerals, and she frowns on ninety-nine out of a hundred picnics.
Dreamthorp

Adlai E(wing) Stevenson
Nature is neutral. Man has wrested from nature the power to make the world a desert or to make the deserts bloom. There is no evil in the atom; only in men's souls.
Speech, 1952

Alfred, Lord Tennyson
Nature red in tooth and claw.
In Memoriam

Henry David Thoreau
We need the tonic of wildness…We can never have enough of nature.
Walden

Voltaire [François Marie Arouet]
Men arge, nature acts.
Philosophical Dictionary

Mary Wollstonecraft
It is the preservation of the species, not of individuals, which appears to be the design of Deity throughout the whole of nature.
Letters written in Sweden, Norway and Denmark

Time & Eternity

Francis Bacon
And he that will not apply New Remedies, must expect New Evils; for Time is the greatest Innovator.
Essays: Of Innovations

The Bible
To everything there is a season, and a time to every purpose under the heaven: A time to be born, and a time to die; a time to plant, and a time to pluck up that which is planted; A time to kill, and a time to heal; a time to break down, and a time to build up; A time to weep, and a time to laugh; a time to mourn, and a time to dance; A time to cast away stones, and a time to gather stones together; a time to embrace, and a time to refrain from embracing; A time to get, and a time to lose; a time to keep, and a time to cast away; A time to rend, and a time to sew; a time to keep silence, and a time to speak; A time to love, and a time to hate; A time of war, and a time of peace.
Ecclesiastes 3

William Blake
To see a world in a grain of sand,
  And heaven in a wild flower,
Hold infinity in the palm of your hand,
  And eternity in an hour.
Auguries of Innocence

Robert Browning
Who knows but the world may end tonight?
  The Last Ride Together

Thomas Carlyle
The illimitable, silent, never-resting thing called Time, rolling,

rushing on, swift, silent, like an all embracing ocean-tide, on which we and all the Universe swim like exhalations.
Heroes and Hero Worship

Julia Fletcher Carney
Little drops of water, little grains of sand,
Make the mighty ocean and the pleasant land.
So the little minutes, humble though they be,
Make the mighty ages of eternity.
Little Things

Philip Dormer Stanhope, 4th Earl of Chesterfield
I recommend you to take care of the minutes, for hours will take care of themselves.
Letters to His Son

Know the true value of time; snatch, seize and enjoy every moment of it. No idleness, no laziness, no procrastination.
Ibid

Sir Noel (Pierce) Coward
Time is the reef upon which all our frail mystic ships are wrecked.
Blithe Spirit

I don't give a hoot about posterity. Why should I worry about what people think of me when I'm dead as a doornail anyway.
Present Laughter

Charles Dickens
It was the best of times, it was the worst of times, it was the age of wisdom, it was the age of foolishness, it was the epoch of belief, it was the epoch of incredulity, it was the season of Light, it was the season of Darkness, it was the spring of hope, it was the winter of despair, we had everything before us, we had nothing before us, we were all going direct to Heaven, we were all going direct the other way.
A Tale of Two Cities

Benjamin Disraeli, 1st Earl of Beaconsfield
Time is the great physician.
Endymion

Sir Francis Drake
There's plenty of time to win this game, and to thrash the Spaniards too. [Sighting of the Armada while playing bowls, 1588.]

John Dryden
A very merry, dancing, drinking,
Laughing, quaffing, and unthinking time.
  Secular Masque

Ralph Waldo Emerson
A day is a miniature eternity.
  Journals

Euripides
Time will reveal everything. It is a babbler, and speaks even when not asked.
  Fragment

Edward FitzGerald
The Bird of Time has but a little way
To fly—and Lo! the Bird is on the Wing.
  The Rubaiyat of Omar Khayyam

Benjamin Franklin
Dost thou love life? Then do not squander time, for that's the stuff life is made of.
  Poor Richard's Almanack 1746

Lost time is never found again.
  Ibid 1748

Remember that time is money.
  Advice to a Young Tradesman

Robert Herrick
Gather ye rosebuds while ye may,
  Old Time is still a-flying:
And this same flower that smiles today,
  Tomorrow will be dying.
  Hesperides: To the Virgins, to Make Much of Time

Mark Antony de Wolfe Howe

Now, thieving Time, take what you must...
Yet leave, O leave exempt from plunder
My curiosity, my wonder!
  Thieving Time

Jean de La Bruyère

Those who make the worse use of their time are the first to complain
of its brevity.
  Caractères

C(live) S(taples) Lewis

The Future is something which everyone reaches at the rate of sixty
minutes an hour, whatever he does, whoever he is.
  The Screwtape Letters

Lucretius

Summarum summa est aeternum.
The sum of all sums is eternity.
  De Natura Rerum

Andrew Marvell

But at my back I always hear
Time's wingèd chariot drawing near.
  To his Coy Mistress

W(illiam) Somerset Maugham

It is bad enough to know the past; it would be intolerable to know
the future.
  Foreign Devil by Richard Hughes

John Milton

Time, the subtle thief of youth.
  Sonnets 7

Friedrich Wilhelm Nietzsche

All things return eternally, and ourselves with them: we have already
existed times without number, and all things with us.
  Thus Spake Zarathustra

Ovid [Publius Ovidius Naso]
Tempus fugit.
Time flies.
  Fasti

Tempus edax rerum.
Time the devourer of all things.
  Metamorphoses

Thomas Paine
These are the times that try men's souls.
  The American Crisis

Pliny the Younger
The happier the time, the faster it goes.
  Letters

Marcel Proust
The time which we have at our disposal every day is elastic; the
passions that we feel expand it, those that we inspire contract it; and
habit fills up what remains.
  Remembrance of Things Past

Will(iam Penn Adair) Rogers
Half our life is spent trying to find something to do with the time we
have rushed through life trying to save.
  The Autobiography of Will Rogers

Sir Walter Scott
There's a gude time coming.
  Rob Roy

Seneca
Veritatem dies aperit.
Time discovers the truth.
  De Ira

William Shakespeare
O, call back yesterday, bid time return.
  King Richard II 3

Time travels in divers paces with divers persons. I'll tell you who
Time ambles withal, who Time trots withal, who Time gallops withal
and who he stands still withal.
  As You Like It 3

For who would bear the whips and and scorns of time.
  Hamlet 3

Tomorrow, and tomorrow, and tomorrow,
Creeps in this petty pace from day to day
To the last syllable of recorded time.
  Troilus and Cressida 5

Samuel Smiles
Those who have most to do, and are willing to work, will find the
most time.
  Self-Help

Herbert Spencer
Time: that which man is always trying to kill, but which ends in
killing him.
  Definitions

Henry David Thoreau
As if you could kill time without injuring eternity.
  Walden

Virgil [Publius Vergilius Maro]
Sed fugit interea, fugit inreparabile tempus.
Time meanwhile flies, flies never to return.
  Georgics

Love

Jane Austen
All the privilege I claim for my own sex…is that of loving longest, when existence or when hope is gone.
Persuasion

Sir J(ames) M(atthew) Barrie
Let no one who loves be called altogether unhappy. Even love unreturned has its rainbow.
The Little Minister

Aphra Behn
Love ceases to be a pleasure when it ceases to be a secret.
The Lover's Watch: Four o'clock

The Bible
And Jacob served seven years for Rachel; and they seemed unto him but a few days, for the love he had to her.
Genesis 29

[Jonathan] thy love to me was wonderful, passing the love of women.
2 Samuel 1

Stay me with flagons, comfort me with apples: for I am sick of love.
Song of Solomon 2

A new commandment I give unto you, That ye love one another; as I have loved you, that ye also love one another.
John 13

Ambrose (Gwinett) Bierce
Love: a temporary insanity curable by marriage or by removal of the patient from the influences under which he incurred the disorder.
The Devil's Dictionary

William Blake

Love seeketh not itself to please,
Nor for itself hath any care,
But for another gives its ease,
And builds a heaven in hell's despair.
   Songs of Experience: The Clod and the Pebble

Ancius Manlius Severinus Boethius

Who can give a law to lovers? Love is a greater law unto itself.
   De Consolatione Philosophiae

Elizabeth Barrett Browning

Unless you can muse in a crowd all day
   On the absent face that fixed you;
Unless you can love, as the angels may,
   With the breadth of heaven betwixt you;
Unless you can dream that his faith is fast,
   Through behoving and unbehoving;
Unless you can die when the dream is past—
   Oh, never call it loving!
   A Woman's Shortcomings

How do I love thee? Let me count the ways.
   Sonnets from the Portugese

Robert Burns

But to see her was to love her,
Love but her, and love for ever.
   Ae Fond Kiss

O, my luve is like a red red rose,
   That's newly sprung in June.
   A Red Red Rose

Samuel Butler

'Tis better to have loved and lost than never to have lost at all.
   The Way of All Flesh

George Gordon (Noel), 6th Lord Byron

Man's love is of man's life a thing apart,

'Tis woman's whole existence.
Don Juan

Lewis Carroll [Charles Lutwidge Dodgson]
And the moral of that is— "Oh, 'tis love, 'tis love that makes the
world go round."
Alice's Adventures in Wonderland

Geoffrey Chaucer
Love is blind.
The Canterbury Tales: The Merchant's Tale

Samuel Taylor Coleridge
A person once said to me that he could make nothing of love, except
that it was friendship accidently combined with desire. Whence I
concluded that he had never been in love.
Table-Talk

William Congreve
Heav'n has no rage like love to hatred turn'd,
Nor Hell a fury like a woman scorn'd.
The Mourning Bride

If there's delight in love, 'tis when I see
That heart, which others bleed for, bleed for me.
The Way of the World

Noel (Pierce) Coward
Mother love, particularly in America, is a highly respected and much
publicized emotion and when exacerbated by gin and bourbon it can
become extremely formidable.
Future Indefinite

Benjamin Disraeli, 1st Earl of Beaconsfield
The magic of first love is our ignorance that it can ever end.
Henrietta Temple

We are all born for love; it is the principle of existence and its only
end.
Sybil

John Donne
For God's sake hold your tongue and let me love.
  The Canonization

Lord Alfred Douglas
I am the love that dare not speak its name. [Homosexual love.]
  Two Loves

John Dryden
Love's the noblest frailty of the mind.
  The Indian Emperor

Pains of love be sweeter far
Than all other pleasures are.
  Tyrannic Love

Edward VIII
I have found it impossible to carry the heavy burden of responsibility
and to discharge my duties as king as I would wish to do without the
help and support of the woman I love.
  Radio broadcast, 11 Dec. 1936

Ralph Waldo Emerson
All mankind love a lover.
  Essays: Love

Henry Fielding
Devil take me, if I think anything but love to be the object of love.
  Amelia

Christopher (Harris) Fry
Oh, the unholy mantrap of love!
  The Lady's not for Burning

John Gay
She who has never lov'd, has never liv'd.
  The Captives

Oliver Goldsmith
Friendship is a disinterested commerce between equals; love, an

abject intercourse between tyrants and slaves.
The Good-Natured Man

Thomas Hardy
A lover without indiscretion is no lover at all.
The Hand of Ethelberta

Nathaniel Hawthorne
Selfishness is one of the qualities apt to inspire love. This might be
thought out at great length.
American Note-Books

James Hogg
O, love, love, love; Love is like a dizziness;
It winna let a poor body gang about his business!
Love is Like a Dizziness

Victor (Marie) Hugo
The supreme happiness of life is the conviction that we are loved.
Les Misérables

Jerome K(lapka) Jerome
Love is like the measles; we all have to go through it.
Idle Thoughts of an Idle Fellow: On Being in Love

Douglas William Jerrold
Love's like the measles—all the worse when it comes late in life.
A Philanthropist

Dr Samuel Johnson
Love is the wisdom of the fool and the folly of the wise.
Johnsonian Miscellanies

John Keats
La belle Dame sans Merci
Hath thee in thrall!
La Belle Dame Sans Merci

François, Duc de La Rochefoucauld
True love is like ghosts, which everybody talks about but few have seen.
Maxims

The pleasure of love is in loving. We are happier in the passion we feel than in that we arouse.
Ibid

Henry Wadsworth Longfellow
There is nothing holier, in this life of ours, than the first consciousness of love—the first fluttering of its silken wings.
Hyperion

Christopher Marlowe
Where both deliberate, the love is slight;
Whoever loved that loved not at first sight?
Hero and Leander

Come live with me, and be my love.
The Passionate Shepherd to His Love

H(enry) L(ouis) Mencken
To be in love is merely to be in a state of perpetual anaesthesis—to mistake an ordinary young man for a Greek god or an ordinary young woman for a goddess.
Prejudices

Molière [Jean-Baptiste Poquelin]
On est aisement dupé par ce qu'on aime.
We are easily duped by those we love.
Le Tartuffe

Thomas Moore
But there's nothing half so sweet in life
As love's young dream.
Irish Melodies: Love's Young Dream

Napoleon I [Napoleon Bonaparte]
I have never loved anyone for love's sake, except, perhaps Josephine—a little.
To Gaspard Gourgaud, St Helena, 1817

Friedrich Wilhelm Nietzsche
Love is the state in which man sees things most decidedly as they are not.
The Antichrist

Dorothy (Rothschild) Parker
Life is a glorious cycle of song
A medley of extemporania,
And love is a thing that can never go wrong
And I am Marie of Rumania.

Blaise Pascal
Le coeur a ses raisons que la raison ne connait point.
The heart has its reasons, of which reason knows nothing.
  Pensées

Alexander Pope
Love, free as air, at sight of human ties,
Spreads his light wings, and in a moment flies.
  Eloisa to Abelard

Jean Paul Richter
Love diminishes the delicacy of women and increases that of men.
  Titan

Samuel Rogers
Oh, she was good as she was fair!
  None—none on earth above her!
As pure in thought as angels are,
  To know her was to love her.
  Jacqueline

Bertrand (Arthur William) Russell, 3rd Earl Russell
To fear love is to fear life, and those who fear life are already three
parts dead.
  Marriage and Morals

Alexander Scott
Luve is ane fervent fire,
Kendillit without desire:
Short plesour, lang displesour,
Repentance is the hire.
  Lo! What it is to Luve

Sir Walter Scott
True love's the gift which God has given
To man alone beneath the heaven.
   The Lay of the Last Minstrel

William Shakespeare
Love comforteth like sunshine after rain,
But Lust's effect is tempest after sun;
Love's gentle spring doth always fresh remain,
Lust's winter comes ere summer half be done:
   Love surfeits not, Lust like a glutton dies;
   Love is all truth, Lust full of forged lies.
   Venus and Adonis

And when Love speaks, the voice of all the gods
Make heaven drowsy with the harmony.
   Love's Labour's Lost 4

A pair of star-cross'd lovers.
   Romeo and Juliet, Prologue

O, swear not by the moon, the inconstant moon,
That monthly changes in her circled orb,
Lest that thy love prove likewise variable.
   Ibid

The course of true love never did run smooth.
   A Midsummer Night's Dream 1

Speak low, if you speak love.
   Much Ado About Nothing 2

If thou remember'st not the slightest folly
That ever love did make thee run into,
Thou hast not loved.
   As You Like It 2

   Down on your knees,
And thank heaven, fasting, for a good man's love.
   Ibid 3

No sooner met but they looked, no sooner looked but they loved, no

sooner loved but they sighed, no sooner sighed but they asked one
another the reason, no sooner knew the reason but they sought the
remedy.
  Ibid 5

Love sought is good, but given unsought is better.
  Twelfth Night 3

Doubt thou the stars are fire;
  Doubt that the sun doth move;
Doubt truth to be a liar;
  But never doubt I love.
  Hamlet 2

  To be wise and love
Exceeds man's might.
  Troilus and Cressida 3

She loved me for the dangers I had pass'd,
And I loved her that she did pity them.
 This only is the witchcraft I have used.
  Othello 1

  Then must you tell
Of one that loved not wisely but too well.
  Ibid 5

There's beggary in the love that can be reckon'd.
  Antony And Cleopatra 1

George Bernard Shaw
When we want to read of the deeds that are done for love, whither do
we turn? To the murder column.
  Three Plays for Puritans, Preface

Percy Bysshe Shelley
The wise want love; and those who love want wisdom.
  Prometheus Unbound

Sir Philip Sidney
My true love hath my heart and I have his,

By just exchange one for the other given.
Arcadia

Sophocles
Love, unconquered in battle.
Antigone

Edmund Spenser
And all for love, and nothing for reward.
The Faerie Queen

Laurence Sterne
Love, an' please your Honour, is exactly like war, in this; that a soldier, though he has escaped three weeks complete o' Saturday night,—may, nevertheless, be shot through his heart on Sunday morning.
Tristram Shandy

Alfred, Lord Tennyson
In the Spring a young man's fancy lightly turns to thoughts of love.
Locksley Hall

He will hold thee, when his passion shall have spent its novel force,
Something better than his dog, a little dearer than his horse.
Ibid

'Tis better to have loved and lost
Than never to have loved at all.
In Memoriam

William Makepeace Thackeray
Some cynical Frenchman has said that there are two parties to a love transaction; the one who loves and the other who condescends to be so treated.
Vanity Fair

Anthony Trollope
There is no happiness in love, except at the end of an English novel.
Barchester Towers

LOVE

Those who have courage to love should have courage to suffer.
  The Bertrams

Royall Tyler
The chains of love are never so binding as when the links are made
of gold.
  The Contrast

Virgil [Publius Vergilius Maro]
Omnia vincit amor.
Love conquers all.

George John Whyte-Melville
We always believe our first love is our last, and our last love our
first.
  Katerfekto

Oscar (Fingall O'Flahertie Wills) Wilde
To love oneself is the beginning of a lifelong romance, Phipps.
  An Ideal Husband

Sex & Chastity

Woody Allen [Allen Stewart Konigsberg]
Don't knock it [masturbation], it's sex with someone you love.

Maxwell Anderson
Virginity is rather a state of mind.
Elizabeth the Queen

St Augustine of Hippo
Da mihi castitatem et continentiam, sed noli modo.
Give me chastity and continence, but not yet.
Confessions

Charles Baudelaire
Sexuality is the lyricism of the masses.
Journaux intimes 93

Francis Beaumont and **John Fletcher**
Kiss till the cow comes home.
The Scornful Lady

Anthony Burgess [John Burgess Wilson]
He said it was artificial respiration but now I find I'm to have his child.
Inside Mr Enderby

George Gordon (Noel), 6th Lord Byron
What men call gallantry, and gods adultery,
Is much more common where the climate's sultry.
Don Juan

Mrs Patrick Campbell
I don't mind where people make love, so long as they don't do it on the street and frighten the horses.
Attributed

Barbara Cartland
I'll wager that in 10 years it will be fashionable again to be a virgin.
The Observer, 'Sayings of the Week', 20 June 1976

I said 10 years ago that in 10 years time it would be smart to be a virgin. Now everyone is back to virgins again.
The Observer, 'Sayings of the Week', 12 July 1987

Gaius Valerius Catullus
Give me a thousand kisses, then a hundred, then another thousand, then a second hundred, then yet another thousand, then a hundred.
Carmin

Philip Dormer Stanhope, 4th Earl of Chesterfield
The pleasure is momentary, the position ridiculous and the expense damnable
Nature 1970

Charles Dickens
I might keep up with a young 'ooman o' large property as hadn't a title, if she made wery fierce love to me. Not else.
Pickwick Papers

John Donne
  Licence my roving hands, and let them go,
Before, behind, between, above, below.
O my America! my new-found-land,
My kingdom, safeliest when with one man mann'd.
  'To his Mistress Going to Bed'

  Full nakedness! All joys are due to thee,
As souls unbodied, bodies uncloth'd must be,
To taste whole joys.
  Ibid

John Dryden
Let not his hand within your bosom stray,
And rudely with your pretty bubbies play.
Imitations of Ovid: Amores

Germaine Greer
No sex is better than bad sex.
  Attributed

Dr Samuel Johnson
Marriage has many pains, but celibacy has no pleasures.
  Rasselas

Juvenal [Decimus Junius Juvenalis]
To set your neighbour's bed a-shaking is now an ancient and long-established custom. It was the silver age which saw the first adulterers.
  Satires

D(avid) H(erbert) Lawrence
You mustn't think I advocate perpetual sex. Far from it. Nothing nauseates me more than promiscuous sex in and out of season. [Referring to *Lady Chatterley's Lover*.]
  Letter to Lady Ottoline Morrell, 22 Dec. 1928

Frédérick Leboyer
Making love is the sovereign remedy for anguish.
  Birth without Violence

Lord Longford
No sex without responsibility.
  The Observer, 3 May 1954

Maimonides [Moses ben Maimon]
He who immerses himself in sexual intercourse will be assailed by premature ageing, his strength will wane, his eyes will weaken, and a bad odour will emit from his mouth and his armpits, his teeth will fall out and many other maladies will afflict him.
  Mishreh Torah

Christopher Marlowe
Thou hast committed—
Fornication: but that was in another country;
and besides, the wench is dead.
  The Jew of Malta

John Masefield
The new lust gives the lecher the new thrill.
   Widow in the Bye Street

George Mikes
Continental people have sex lives. The English have hot water
bottles.
   How To Be An Alien

Henry Miller
Sex is one of the nine reasons for reincarnation...The other eight are
unimportant.
   Big Sur and the Oranges of Hieronymus Bosch

Lord Montgomery
This sort of thing [homosexuality] may be tolerated by the French
but we are British—thank God.
   Daily Mail, 27 May 1965

J. Earle Moore
Two minutes with Venus, two years with mercury.
   Aphorism

Thomas Moore
Then awake!—the heavens look bright, my dear,
'Tis never too late for delight, my dear,
   And the best of all ways
   To lengthen our days,
Is to steal a few hours from the night, my dear!
   Irish Melodies: The Young May Moon

Ovid [Publius Ovidius Naso]
Arte perennat amor.
Skill makes love unending.
   Ars Amatoria

Cynthia Payne
I know it does make people happy but to me it is just like having a
cup of tea.
   Said 8 Nov. 1987

Thomas Shadwell
'Tis the way of all flesh.
The Sullen Lovers

William Shakespeare
Is it not strange that desire should so many years outlive performance?
Henry IV, Part II 2

Your daughter and the Moor are now making the beast with two backs.
Othello 1

I'll canvass thee between a pair of sheets.
II Henry IV 2

Graze on my lips, and if those hills be dry,
Stray lower, where the pleasant fountains lie.
Venus and Adonis

Thomas Szasz
Masturbation: the primary sexual activity of mankind. In the nineteenth century it was a disease; in the twentieth it's a cure.
The Second Sin.

Henry David Thoreau
I lose my respect for the man who can make the mystery of sex the subject of a coarse joke, yet, when you speak earnestly and seriously on the subject, is silent.
Journal, 12 April 1852

Mary Day Winn
Sex is the tabasco sauce which an adolescent national palate sprinkles on every course in the menu.
Adam's Rib

Marriage

Susan B(rownell) Anthony

Marriage, to women as to men, must be a luxury, not a necessity; an incident of life, not all of it. And the only possible way to accomplish this great change is to accord to women equal power in the making, shaping and controlling of the circumstances of life.

   Speech, 1875

Aristophanes

A man, though he be grey-haired, can always get a wife. But a woman's time is short.

   Lysistrata

Jane Austen

Happiness in marriage is entirely a matter of chance.

   Pride and Prejudice

Lord, how ashamed I should be of not being married before three and twenty!

   Ibid

Francis Bacon

Wives are young men's mistresses; companions for middle age; and old men's nurses.

   Essays: Of Marriage and Single Life

Honoré de Balzac

No man should marry until he has studied anatomy and dissected at least one woman.

   The Physiology of Marriage

Being a husband is a whole-time job. That is why so many husbands fail. They cannot give their entire attention to it.

   The Title

So long as there are differences between one moment of pleasure and another a man can go on being happy with the same woman.
  The Physiology of Marriage

The Bible

I say therefore to the unmarried and widows, It is good for them if they abide even as I. But if they cannot contain, let them marry: for it is better to marry than to burn.
  1 Corinthians 7

Ambrose (Gwinett) Bierce

Marriage: the state or condition of a community consisting of a master, a mistress and two slaves, making in all, two.
  The Devil's Dictionary

Wedding: a ceremony at which two persons undertake to become one, one undertakes to become nothing, and nothing undertakes to become supportable.
  Ibid

Robert Burton

One was never married, and that's his hell; another is, and that's his plague.
  The Anatomy of Melancholy

Mrs Patrick Campbell

Marriage is the result of the longing for the deep, deep peace of the double bed after the hurly-burly of the chaise longue.
  Attributed

Sir Winston (Leonard Spencer) Churchill

Lady Astor: If I were your wife, I should flavour your coffee with poison!
Sir Winston: And If I were your husband, madam, I should drink it.
  Attributed

Marcus Tullius Cicero

The first bond of society is marriage.
  De Officiis

Charles Caleb Colton
Marriage is a feast where the grace is sometimes better than the dinner.
Lacon

William Congreve
Courtship to marriage, as a very witty prologue to a very dull play.
The Old Bachelor

Married in haste, we may repent at leisure.
Ibid

Charles Dickens
Wen you're a married man, Samivel, you'll understand a good many things as you don't understand now; but vether it's worth while goin' through so much to learn so little, as the charity boy said ven he got to the end of the alphabet, is a matter o' taste.
Pickwick Papers

Benjamin Disraeli, 1st Earl of Beaconsfield
I have always thought that every woman should marry, and no man.
Lothair

Marriage is the greatest earthly happiness when founded on complete sympathy.
Letter to Gladstone

John Dryden
Here lies my wife: here let her lie,
Now she's at rest, and so am I.
Epitaph Intended for Dryden's Wife

Benjamin Franklin
Where there's marriage without love, there will be love without marriage.
Poor Richard's Almanack 1734

John Gay
Do you think your mother and I should have liv'd comfortably so

long together, if ever we had been married?
  The Beggar's Opera

Sir A(lan) P(atrick) Herbert
The critical period in matrimony is breakfast time.
  Uncommon Law

Hesiod
Marry in the springtime of thy life, neither much above or below the age of thirty. Thy wife should be a virgin in her nineteenth year.
  Works and Days

Rudyard Kipling
The bachelor may risk 'is 'ide
  To 'elp you when you're downed;
But the married man will wait beside
  Till the ambulance comes round.
  The Married Man

Abraham Lincoln
Marriage is neither heaven nor hell. It is simply purgatory.
  Attributed, 1864

Henry Wadsworth Longfellow
The men that women marry,
And why they marry them, will always be
A marvel and a mystery to the world.
  Michael Angelo

Sir (Edward Morgan) Compton Mackenzie
Prostitution. Selling one's body to keep one's soul…one might say of most marriages that they were selling one's soul to keep one's body.
  The Adventures of Sylvia Scarlett

Menander
Marriage, to tell the truth, is an evil, but it is a necessary evil.
  Fragment

Molière [Jean-Baptiste Poquelin]
Marriage, Agnes, is not a joke.
  L'Ecole des femmes

Thomas Moore
It is time you should think, boy, of taking a wife—"
"Why, so it is, father—whose wife shall I take?"
  A Joke Versified

Thomas Love Peacock
Love is to be avoided because marriage is at best a dangerous
experiment.
  Gryll Grange

Bertrand (Arthur William) Russell, 3rd Earl Russell
The more civilized people become the less capable they seem of
lifelong happiness with one partner.
  Marriage and Morals

Saki [Hector Hugh Munro]
The Western custom of one wife and hardly any mistresses.
  Reginald in Russia

William Shakespeare
Many a good hanging prevents a bad marriage.
  Twelfth Night 1

A young man married is a man that's marr'd.
  All's Well That Ends Well 2

George Bernard Shaw
Marriage…combines the maximum of temptation with the maximum
of opportunity.
  Man and Superman: Maxims for Revolutionists

Percy Bysshe Shelley
When a man marries, dies or turns Hindoo,
His best friends hear no more of him.
  Letter to Maria Gisborne

A system could not well have been devised more studiously hostile to human happiness than marriage.

Queen Mab, Notes

Richard Brinsley Sheridan

'Tis safest in matrimony to begin with a little aversion.

The Rivals

Robert Louis Stevenson

Marriage is like life in this—that it is a field of battle, and not a bed of roses.

Ibid

In marriage, a man becomes slack and selfish, and undergoes a fatty degenertion of his moral being.

Ibid

Publilius Syrus

It is mind, not body, that makes marriage last.

Sententiae

William Makepeace Thackeray

Remember, it's as easy to marry a rich woman as a poor woman.

Pendennis

Oscar (Fingall O'Flahertie Wills) Wilde

Twenty years of romance make a woman look like a ruin; but twenty years of marriage make her something like a public building.

A Woman of No Importance

Thornton (Niven) Wilder

The best part of married life is the fights. The rest is merely so-so.

The Matchmaker

Home & Hearth

(Amos) Bronson Alcott
As the homes, so the state.
  Tablets

Jane Austen
A family of ten children will always be called a fine family, where
there are heads, and arms, and legs enough for that number.
  Northanger Abbey

Francis Bacon
He that hath wife and children, hath given hostages to fortune; for
they are impediments to great enterprises, either of virtue or mischief.
  Essays: Of Marriage and Single Life

Nicholas Breton
He that lives at home, sees nothing but home.
  Works

Robert Burns
To make a happy fireside clime
        To weans and wife,
That's the true pathos and sublime
        Of human life.
  Epistle to Dr Blacklock

Miguel de Cervantes (Saavedra)
You are a king by your own fireside, as much as any monarch in his
throne.
  Don Quixote

Whom God loves, his house is sweet to him.
  Ibid

Marcus Tullius Cicero
Nullus est locus domestica sede jucundior.

No place is more delightful than one's own fireside.
Epistolæ ad Familiares

Samuel Taylor Coleridge
The largest part of mankind are nowhere greater strangers than at home.
Table Talk

William Cowper
Domestic happiness, Thou only bliss
Of Paradise that has surviv'd the fall!
The Task: The Garden

Sir John Davies
Every groom is a king at home.
The Scourge of Folly

Charles Dickens
Home is home, be it ever so homely.
Dombey and Son

Phineas Fletcher
A saint abroad, at home a fiend.
The Purple Island

Robert (Lee) Frost
Home is the place where, when you have to go there,
They have to take you in.
The Death of the Hired Man

Mrs Elizabeth Cleghorn Gaskell
A man is so in the way in the house.
Cranford

Oliver Goldsmith
I am now no more than a mere lodger in my own house.
The Good-Natured Man 1

Thomas Jefferson
The happiest moments of my life have been the few which I have

passed at home in the bosom of my family.
   Letter, 1790

The happiness of the domestic fireside is the first boon of Heaven;
and it is well it is so, since it is that which is the lot of the mass of
mankind.
   Ibid, 1813

F. M. Knowles
There's no place like home, and many a man is glad of it.
   A Cheerful Year Book

Christopher Morley
Joy dwells beneath a humble roof;
Heaven is not built of country seats
But little queer suburban streets.
   To the Little House

John Howard Payne
'Mid pleasures and palaces though we may roam,
Be it ever so humble, there's no place like home.
   Clari, the Maid of Milan

Samuel Pepys
Home, and, being washing day, dined upon cold meat.
   Diary, 4 April 1666

Pliny the Elder
Home is where the heart is.
   Attributed

Alexander Pope
I find that by all you have been telling,
That 'tis a house, but not a dwelling.
   On the Duke of Marlborough's House

Samuel Rogers
To fireside happiness, to hours of ease,
Blest with that charm, the certainty to please.
   Human Life

William Shakespeare
As 'tis ever common
That men are merriest when they are from home.
King Henry V 1

George Bernard Shaw
Home is the girl's prison and the woman's workhouse.
Man and Superman: Maxims for Revolutionists

Home life as we understand it is no more natural to us than a cage is
natural to a cockatoo.
Getting Married

Dodie Smith
That dear octopus from whose tentacles we never quite escape, nor
in our innermost hearts never quite wish to.
Dear Octopus

Sydney Smith
A comfortable house is a great source of happiness. It ranks
immediately after health and a good conscience.
Letter to Lord Murray, 29 Sept. 1843

Women

Anacreon
Nature gave horns to bulls, hooves to horses, speed to hares, the power of swimming to fishes, that of flying to birds, and understanding to men. She had nothing left to give to women save beauty.
  Fragment

Simone de Beauvoir
One is not born a woman, one becomes one.
  The Second Sex

It is in great part the anxiety of being a woman that devastates the feminine body.
  Womansize by Kim Chernin

Sir Max Beerbohm
"After all," as a pretty girl once said to me, "women are a sex by themselves, so to speak."
  The Pervasion of Rouge

The Bible
Favour is deceitful, and beauty is vain: but a woman that feareth the Lord, she shall be praised.
  Proverbs 31

Philip Dormer Stanhope, 4th Earl of Chesterfield
Women are much more like each other than men: they have, in truth, but two passions, vanity and love.
  Letters to His Son

Hannah Cowley
What is woman?—only one of Nature's agreeable blunders.
  Who's the Dupe!

Edwina Currie
The strongest possible piece of advice I would give to any young woman is: Don't screw around and don't smoke.
  The Observer, 'Sayings of the Week', 3 April 1988

Christian Dior
Women are most fascinating between the ages of thirty-five and forty, after they have won a few races and know how to pace themselves. Since few women ever pass forty, maximum fascination can continue indefinitely.
  Colliers Magazine, 10 June 1955

George Eliot [Mary Ann Evans]
I'm not denyin' the women are foolish: God Almighty made 'em to match the men.
  Adam Bede

I should like to know what is the proper function of women, if it is not to make reasons for husbands to stay at home, and still stronger reasons for bachelors to go out.
  The Mill on the Floss

The happiest women, like the happiest nations, have no history.
  Ibid

Elizabeth I
I know I have the body of a weak and feeble woman, but I have the heart and stomach of a king, and of a king of England too.
  Speech, 1588

George Farquhar
How a little love and good company improves a woman.
  The Beaux' Stratagem

Sigmund Freud
What does a woman want?

Betty (Naomi) Friedan
It is easier to live through someone else than to become complete yourself.
  The Feminine Mystique

Erich Fromm
Women are equal because they are not different any more.
The Art of Loving

Thomas Hardy
Time and circumstance, which enlarge the views of most men,
narrow the views of women almost invariably.
Jude the Obscure

Juvenal [Decimus Junius Juvenalis]
Nothing is more intolerable than a wealthy woman.
Satires

John Keats
I have met with women whom I really think would like to be married
to a poem, and to be given away by a novel.
Letter, 1819

François, Duc de La Rochefoucauld
One can find women who have never had a love affair, but it is rare
to find a woman who has had only one.
Maxims

Groucho (Julius Henry) Marx
You're the most beautiful woman I've ever seen, which doesn't say
much for you.
Animal Crackers

Friedrich Wilhelm Nietzsche
God created woman. And boredom did indeed cease from that
moment—but many other things ceased as well! Woman was God's
second mistake.
The Antichrist

In revenge, as in love, woman is always more barbarous than man.
Beyond Good and Evil

Woman likes to believe that love can achieve anything. It is her
peculiar superstition.
Ibid

When a woman becomes a scholar there is usually something wrong
with her sexual organs.
   In *Bartlett's Unfamiliar Quotations*

Thomas Otway
O woman! lovely woman! Nature made thee
To temper man: we had been brutes without you.
   Venice Preserv'd

Arthur Schopenhauer
Women exist in the main solely for the propagation of the species.

Sir Walter Scott
O Woman! in our hours of ease,
Uncertain, coy, and hard to please…
When pain and anguish wring the brow
A ministering angel thou!
   Marmion: Lochinvar

William Makepeace Thackeray
'Tis strange what a man may do, and a woman yet think him an
angel.
   The History of Henry Esmond

This I set down as a positive truth. A woman with fair opportunities
and without an absolute hump, may marry whom she likes.
   Vanity Fair

Margaret (Hilda) Thatcher
No woman in my time will be Prime Minister or Chancellor or
Foreign Secretary—not the top jobs.
   The Sunday Telegraph, 1969

Oscar (Fingall O'Flahertie Wills) Wilde
Women have become so highly educated that nothing should surprise
them except happy marriages.
   A Woman of No Importance

All women become like their mothers. That is their tragedy. No man
does. That is his.
   Ibid

Parents & Offspring

Anonymous
The law of heredity is that all undesirable traits come from the other parent.

Francis Bacon
The joys of parents are secret, and so are their griefs and fears.
   Essays: Of Parents and Children

Children sweeten labours, but they make misfortunes more bitter.
   Ibid

The Bible
He that spareth his rod hateth his son: but he that loveth him chasteneth.
   Proverbs 13

The fathers have eaten sour grapes, and the children's teeth are set on edge.
   Ezekiel 18

Lewis Carroll [Charles Lutwidge Dodgson]
Speak roughly to your little boy.
   And beat him when he sneezes:
He only does it to annoy,
   Because he knows it teases.
   Alice's Adventures in Wonderland

Marcus Tullius Cicero
Quid dulcius hominum generi ab natura datum est quam sui cuique liberi?
Of all nature's gifts to the human race, what is sweeter to a man than his children?
   Post Reditum ad Quirites

Mrs Dinah Maria Craik
Oh, my son's my son till he gets him a wife,
But my daughter's my daughter all her life.
Young and Old

Bernard le Bovier de Fontenelle,
The follies of the fathers are no warning to the children.
Dialogues des morts

Benjamin Franklin
"Late children," says the Spanish proverb, "are early orphans."
Letter to John Alleyn

Jean de La Fontaine
It is impossible to please all the world and also one's father.
Fables

William Langland
Whoso spareth the spring spoileth his children.
Piers Plowman

Stephen Butler Leacock
The parent who could see his boy as he really is, would shake his
head and say: "Willie is no good: I'll sell him."
The Lot of the Schoolmaster

Menander
A daughter is an embarrassing and ticklish possession.
Perinthis

Napoleon I [Napoleon Bonaparte]
It is horrible to see oneself die without children.
To Gaspard Gourgaud, St Helena, 1817

John Ray
Children suck the mother when they are young, and the father when
they are grown.
English Proverbs

Samuel Richardson
Children when they are little make parents fools, when great, mad.
Clarissa Harlowe

Sir Walter Scott
A mother's pride, a father's joy.
Rokeby

William Shakespeare
It is a wise father that knows his own child.
The Merchant of Venice 2

How sharper than a serpent's tooth it is
To have a thankless child!
King Lear 1

Laurence Sterne, 1713-68
I wish either my father or my mother, or indeed both of them, as they were in duty both equally bound to it, had minded what they were about when they begot me.
Tristram Shandy

Sir Henry Taylor
A spoilt child never loves its mother.
Notes from Life

Oscar (Fingall O'Flahertie Wills) Wilde
Children begin by loving their parents, After a time they judge them. Rarely, if ever, do they forgive them.
A Woman of No Importance

Travel

Francis Bacon
Travel, in the younger sort, is a part of education; in the elder, a part of experience.
   Essays: Of Travel

Giuseppe Baretti
Travellers…seem to have no other purpose by taking long journeys but to procure themselves the pleasure of railing at everything they have seen or heard.
   An Account of the Manners and Customs of Italy

Sir Thomas Beecham
I have recently been all round the world and have formed a very poor opinion of it.

Fanny Burney [Frances, Madame d'Arblay]
Travelling is the ruin of all happiness. There's no looking at a building here after seeing Italy.
   Cecilia

Albert Camus
There is no pleasure in travelling, and I look upon it more as an occasion for spiritual testing.
   Notebooks

Philip Dormer Stanhope, 4th Earl of Chesterfield
Those who travel heedlessly from place to place, observing only their distance from each other, and attending only to their accommodation at the inn at night, set out fools, and will certainly return so.
   Letters to His Son

René Descartes
Travelling is almost like talking with men of other centuries.
   Le Discours de la Méthode

Benjamin Disraeli, 1st Earl of Beaconsfield
Travel teaches toleration.
  Contarini Fleming

Ralph Waldo Emerson
All educated Americans, first or last, go to Europe.
  The Conduct of Life: Culture

Carlo Goldoni
A wise traveller never despises his own country.
  Pamela Nubile

William Hazlitt
I should like to spend the whole of my life travelling, if I could anywhere borrow another life to spend at home.
  Table Talk

Ernest Hemingway
If you are lucky enough to have lived in Paris as a young man, then wherever you go for the rest of your life, it stays with you, for Paris is a moveable feast.
  A Moveable Feast

Homer
There is nothing worse for mortals than a wandering life.
  Odyssey

James Henry Leigh Hunt
Travelling in the company of those we love is home in motion.
  The Indicator

Juvenal [Decimus Junius Juvenalis]
Travel light and you can sing in the robber's face.
  Satires

Rudyard Kipling
He travels the fastest who travels alone.
  The Winners

Herman Melville
I love to sail forbidden seas, and land on barbarous coasts.
 Moby Dick

Edna St Vincent Millay
My heart is warm with the friends I make,
And better friends I'll not be knowing;
Yet there isn't a train I wouldn't take,
No matter where it's going.
 Travel

Jonathan Raban
In an underdeveloped country don't drink the water, in a developed
country, don't breathe the air.
 Reader's Digest, 1976

John Ruskin
All travelling becomes dull in exact proportion to its rapidity.
 Modern Painters

Seneca
Every change of scene is a delight.
 Epistolæ ad Lucilium

William Shakespeare
Farewell, Monsieur Traveller: look you lisp and wear strange suits,
disable all the benefits of your own country, be out of love with your
nativity, and almost chide God for making you the countenance you
are, or I will scarce think you have swum in a gondola.
 As You Like It 4

Philip Henry Sheridan
If I owned Texas and Hell, I would rent out Texas and live in Hell.
 Said 1855

Laurence Sterne
A man should know something of his own country, too, before he
goes abroad.
 Tristram Shandy

They order, said I, this matter better in France.
   A Sentimental Journey

Robert Louis Stevenson
For my part, I travel not to go anywhere, but to go. I travel for travel's sake. The great affair is to move.
   Travels with a Donkey; Cheylard and Luc

To travel hopefully is a better thing than to arrive.
   Virginibus Puerisque: El Dorado

Wealth I ask not, hope nor love,
Nor a friend to know me;
All I ask, the heaven above
And the road below me.
   Songs of Travel: The Vagabond

Mark Twain [Samuel Langhorne Clemens]
To forget pain is to be painless; to forget care is to rid of it; to go abroad is to accomplish both.
   Autobiography

Sir Laurens Van der Post
I have travelled so much because travel has enabled me to arrive at unknown places within my clouded self.

William Carlos Williams
Most of the beauties of travel are due to the strange hours we keep to see them.
   Selected Poems, 'January Morning'

William Wordsworth
I have travelled among unknown men
   In lands beyond the sea;
Nor, England! did I know till then
   What love I bore to thee.
   I Travelled among Unknown Men

Friendship & Emnity

Henry (Brooks) Adams
A friend in power is a friend lost.
The Education of Henry Adams

Friends are born not made.
Ibid

Aristotle
The perfect friendship is that between good men, alike in their virtue.
The Nicomachean Ethics

Without friends no one would choose to live, though he had all other goods.
Ibid

Francis Bacon
The worst solitude is to be destitute of sincere friendship.
De Augmentis Scientiarum

The Bible
A friend loveth at all times, and a brother is born for adversity.
Proverbs 17

Greater love hath no man than this, that a man lay down his life for his friends.
John 15

A faithful friend is a strong defence: and he that hath found such a one hath found a treasure.
Ecclesiasticus 6

A faithful friend is the medicine of life.
Ibid

Forsake not an old friend; for the new is not comparable to him; a new

friend is as new wine; when it is old, thou shalt drink it with pleasure.
Ibid 9

Ambrose (Gwinett) Bierce
Acquaintance: a person whom we know well enough to borrow from, but not well enough to lend to.
The Devil's Dictionary

Friendless: having no favours to bestow. Destitute of fortune. Addicted to utterance of truth and common sense.
Ibid

Nicholas Breton
I wish my deadly foe no worse
Than want of friends, and empty purse.
A Farewell to Town

"Beau" (George Bryan) Brummell
Who's your fat friend? [Of the Prince of Wales.]

Robert Burns
I want someone to laugh with me, someone to be grave with me, someone to please me and help my discrimination with his or her own remark, and at times, no doubt, to admire my acuteness and penetration.
Commonplace Book

Should auld acquaintance be forgot,
And days o' auld lang syne.
Auld Lang Syne

George Gordon (Noel) Byron, 6th Lord Byron
Friendship is Love without his wings.
Hours of Idleness

George Canning
But of all plagues, good Heaven, thy wrath can send,
Save, save, oh save me from the candid friend!
New Morality

George Chapman
Trust not a reconciled friend, for good turns cannot blot out old grudges.
Alphonsus

Marcus Tullius Cicero
A friend is, as it were, a second self.
De Amicitia

Charles Caleb Colton
Friendship often ends in love; but love, in friendship—never.
Lacon

If you want enemies, excel others; if you want friends, let others excel you.
Ibid

William Cowper
How sweet, how passing sweet, is solitude!
But grant me still a friend in my retreat,
Whom I may whisper—solitude is sweet.
Retirement

Abbé Jacques Delille
Fate chooses our relatives, we choose our friends.
Malheur et Pitié

Charles Dickens
Fan the sinking flame of hilarity with the wing of friendship; and pass the rosy wine.
The Old Curiosity Shop

Wery glad to see you, indeed, and hope our acquaintance may be a long 'un, as the gen'l'm'n said to the fi' pun' note.
Pickwick Papers

George Louis Palmella Busson Du Maurier
I have no talent for making new friends, but oh, such a genius for fidelity to old ones.
Peter Ibbetson

George Eliot [Mary Ann Evans]
Friendships begin with liking or gratitude—roots that can be pulled up.
  Daniel Deronda

Benjamin Franklin
There are three faithful friends—an old wife, an old dog, and ready money.
  Poor Richard's Almanac 1738

William Hazlitt
I like a friend the better for having faults that one can talk about.
  Plain Speaker

Thomas Jefferson
An injured friend is the bitterest of foes.
  French Treaties Opinion

I find friendship to be like wine, raw when new, ripened with age, the true old man's milk and restorative cordial.
  Letter, 1811

Dr Samuel Johnson
If a man does not make new acquaintance as he advances through life, he will soon find himself left alone. A man, sir, should keep his friendship in constant repair.
  Boswell's *Life of Johnson*

Ben Jonson
  True happiness
Consists not in the multitude of friends,
But in the worth and choice.
  Cynthia's Revels

Paul de Kock
The best way to keep your friends is to never borrow from them and never lend them anything.
  Homme aux trois culottes

Leonardo da Vinci
Reprove a friend in secret, but praise him before others.
  Notebooks

Ovid [Publius Ovidius Naso]
The vulgar estimate friends by the advantage to be derived from them.
Epistulæ ex Ponto

Blaise Pascal
I lay it down as a fact that if all men knew what others say of them, there would not be four friends in the world.
Pensées

William Penn
A true friend unbosoms freely, advises justly, assists readily, adventures boldly, takes all patiently, defends courageously, and continues a friend unchangeably.
Some Fruits of Solitude

Alexander Pope
Histories are more full of examples of the fidelity of dogs than of friends.
Letter, 1709

John Selden
Old friends are best. King James used to call for his old shoes; they were easiest for his feet.
Table Talk: Friends

William Shakespeare
I count myself in nothing else so happy
As in a soul remembering my good friends.
King Richard II 2

Our plot is as good a plot as ever was laid; our friends true and constant; a good plot, good friends, and full of expectation; an excellent plot, very good friends.
King Henry IV, Part I 2

Sophocles
An enemy should be hated only so far as one may be hated who may one day be a friend.
Ajax

Alfred, Lord Tennyson
He makes no friend who never made a foe.
  Idylls of the King: Lancelot and Elaine

Mark Twain [Samuel Langhorne Clemens]
The holy passion of Friendship is of so sweet and steady and loyal
and enduring a nature that it will last through a whole lifetime, if not
asked to lend money.
  Pudd'nhead Wilson

Voltaire [François Marie Arouet]
I have never made but one prayer to God, a very short one: "O Lord,
make my enemies ridiculous." And God granted it.
  Letter, 1767

Walt Whitman
I no doubt deserved my enemies, but I don't believe I deserved my
friends.
  Bradford's *Biography and the Human Heart*

Oscar (Fingall O'Flahertie Wills) Wilde
I choose my friends for their good looks, my acquaintances for their
characters, and my enemies for their brains.
  The Picture of Dorian Gray

Edward Young
Friendship's the wine of life.
  Night Thoughts

War & Peace

Lewis Addison Armistead
Give them the cold steel, boys!
  Battle of Gettysburg, 1863

Bernard M(annes) Baruch
We are today in the midst of a cold war.
  To Senate Committee, 1948

Sir John Betjeman
Gracious Lord, oh bomb the Germans.
  In Westminster Abbey

The Bible
How are the mighty fallen, and the weapons of war perished!
  2 Samuel 1

Blessed are the peacemakers: for they shall be called the children of
God.
  Matthew 5

Put up again thy sword into his place: for all they that take the sword
shall perish with the sword.
  Ibid 26

Ambrose (Gwinett) Bierce
Peace: in international affairs, a period of cheating between two
periods of fighting.
  The Devil's Dictionary

Gaius Julius Caesar
In war trivial causes produce momentous events.
  The Gallic War

Sir Winston (Leonard Spencer) Churchill
I cannot forecast to you the action of Russia. It is a riddle wrapped in

a mystery inside an enigma.
   Radio broadcast, 1939

"I have nothing to offer but blood, toil, tears and sweat."
   House of Commons speech, 13 May 1940

We shall not flag or fail. We shall go on to the end, we shall fight in France, we shall fight on the seas and oceans…we shall fight on the beaches, we shall fight on the landing grounds, we shall fight in the fields and in the streets, we shall fight in the hills; we shall never surrender.
   Ibid 4 June 1940

Never in the field of human conflict was so much owed by so many to so few [Battle of Britain pilots].
   Ibid 20 Aug. 1940

Karl von Clausewitz
War is the continuation of politics by other means.
   On War

Ferdinand Foch
Mon centre cède, ma droite recule, situation excellente, j'attaque.
My centre is giving way, my right is pushed back, situation excellent, I am attacking.
   Battle of the Marne, 1914

Benjamin Franklin
There never was a good war or a bad peace.
   Letter, 1773

Oliver Goldsmith
He who fights and runs away
May live to fight another day.
   The Art of Poetry on a New Plan

The first blow is half the battle.
   She Stoops to Conquer

Ulysses S(impson) Grant
The art of war is simple enough. Find out where your enemy is. Get

at him as soon as you can. Strike him as hard as you can and as often
as you can, and keep moving on.
  On the Art of War

Thomas Hobbes
The first and fundamental law of nature…is to seek peace and follow it.
  Leviathan

Oliver Wendell Holmes
The peaceful are the strong.
  A Voice of the Loyal North

Herbert (Clark) Hoover
Older men declare war. But it is youth that must fight and die.
  Speech, 1944

John Paul II [Karol Wojtyla]
War should belong to the tragic past, in history. It should find no
place on humanity's agenda for the future.
  Coventry, 1982

John Fitzgerald Kennedy
Mankind must put an end to war or war will put an end to mankind.
  United Nations, 1961

Rudyard Kipling
For it's Tommy this, an' Tommy that, an' "Chuck him out, the brute!"
But it's "Saviour of 'is country" when the guns begin to shoot.
  Barrack Room Ballads

Henry Wadsworth Longfellow
Buried was the bloody hatchet;
Buried was the dreadful war-club;
Buried were all war-like weapons,
And the war-cry was forgotten,
Then was peace among the nations,
  The Song of Hiawatha

Martin Luther
War is the greatest plague that can afflict humanity; it destroys

religion, it destroys states, it destroys families. Any scourge is preferable to it.
Table Talk

Dr John McCrae
In Flanders fields the poppies blow
Between the crosses, row on row.
In Flanders Fields

Mao Tse-Tung
Politics is war without bloodshed, while war is politics with bloodshed.
Quotations from Chairman Mao

Helmuth Karl Bernard, Count von Moltke
Everlasting peace is a dream, and not even a beautiful one.
Letter, 1880

Napoleon I [Napoleon Bonaparte]
What a beautiful fix we are in now: peace has been declared!
Following Treaty of Amiens, 1802

Frederick, Lord North, 2nd Earl of Guildford
I do not know whether our generals will frighten the enemy, but I know they frighten me whenever I think of them.
Attributed

William Shakespeare
Once more into the breach, dear friends, once more:
Or close the wall up with our English dead!
In peace ther's nothing so becomes a man
As modest stillness and humility:
But when the blast of war blows in our ears,
Then imitate the action of the tiger;
Stiffen the sinews, summon up the blood,
Disguise fair nature with hard-favour'ed rage;
Then lend the eye a terrible aspect.
King Henry V 3

Follow your spirit; and, upon this charge

Cry "God for Harry! England and Saint George!"
  Ibid

O war! thou son of hell!
  II Henry VI 5

Cry, "Havoc," and let slip the dogs of war.
  Julius Caesar 3

Let me have war, say I; it exceeds peace as far as day does night; it's spritely, waking, audible, and full of vent. Peace is a very apoplexy, lethargy: mulled, deaf, sleep, insensible; a getter of more bastard children than war's a destroyer of men.
  Coriolanus 5

William (Tecumseh) Sherman

War is at best barbarism...Its glory is all moonshine. It is only those who have neither fired a shot nor heard the shrieks and groans of the wounded who cry aloud for blood, more vengeance, more desolation. War is hell.
  Attributed, 1879

Peter (Alexander) Ustinov

Generals are fascinating cases of arrested development—after all, at five we all of us wanted to be generals.
  The Illustrated London News, 1968

George Washington

There is nothing so likely to produce peace as to be well prepared to meet an enemy.
  Letter, 1780

Oscar (Fingall O'Flahertie Wills) Wilde

As long as war is regarded as wicked, it will always have its fascination. When it is looked upon as vulgar, it will cease to be popular.
  The Critic as Artist

Health & Sickness

Joseph Addison
Health and cheerfulness mutually beget each other.
  The Spectator, 1712

Anonymous
Get up at five, have lunch at nine,
Super at five, retire at nine.
And you will live to ninety-nine.
  Rabelais's *Works*

Francis Bacon
The remedy is worse than the disease.
  Essays: Of Seditions and Troubles

The Bible
Be not slow to visit the sick.
  Ecclesiasticus 7

Health and good estate of body are above all gold.
  Ibid 30

Sir Thomas Browne
We all labour against our own cure, for death is the cure of all
diseases.
  Religio Medici

Samuel Butler
I reckon being ill as one of the greatest pleasures of life, provided
one is not too ill and is not obliged to work till one is better.
  The Way of All Flesh

Chauncey Depew
I get my exercise acting as a pallbearer to my friends who exercise.
  Attributed

Mary Baker Glover Eddy
Health is not a condition of matter, but of mind.
Science and Health

Ralph Waldo Emerson
A person seldom falls sick, but the bystanders are animated with a faint hope that he will die.
The Conduct of Life: Considerations By the Way

Henry Ford
Exercise is bunk. If you are healthy, you don't need it: if you are sick, you shouldn't take it.
Attributed

Hippocrates
Natural forces within us are the true healers of disease.
Aphorisms

James Gibbons Huneker
My corns ache, I get gouty, and my prejudices swell like varicose veins.
Old Fogy

Dr Samuel Johnson
Disease generally begins that equality which death completes.
The Rambler

How few of his friends' houses would a man choose to be at when sick.
Boswell's *Life of Johnson*

Charles Lamb
What have I gained by health? Intolerable dullness. What by early hours and moderate meals? A total blank.
Letter to Wordsworth, 1830

To be sick is to enjoy monarchal prerogatives.
Last Essays of Elia, 'The Convalescent'.

How sickness enlarges the dimensions of a man's self to himself.
Ibid

François, Duc de La Rochefoucauld
It is a boresome disease to try to keep health by following too strict a regimen.
Maxims

Plato
Attention to health is the greatest hinderance to life.

Alexander Pope
Here am I dying of a hundred good symptoms.
Said to George Lyttleton, 15 May 1744

John Ray
Diseases are the tax on pleasures.
English Proverbs

Jules Romains
Every man who feels well is a sick man neglecting himself.
Knock, ou le triomphe de la médecine

Seneca
It is part of the cure to wish to be cured.
Phaedra

James Thomson
Health is the vital principle of bliss.
The Castle of Indolence

Henry David Thoreau
'Tis healthy to be sick sometimes.

Virgil [Publius Vergilius Maro]
He destroys his health by labouring to preserve it.
Aeneid

Oscar (Fingall O'Flahertie Wills) Wilde
One knows so well the popular idea of health. The English country gentleman galloping after a fox—the unspeakable in full pursuit of the uneatable.
A Woman of No Importance

Doctors & Medicine

The Bible
Honour a physician with the honour due unto him for the uses which
ye may have of him: for the Lord hath created him.
  Ecclesiasticus 38

He that sinneth before his Maker, let him fall into the hand of the
physician.
  Ibid

Physician, heal thyself.
  Luke 4

Ambrose (Gwinett) Bierce
Homeopathy: A school of medicine midway between Allopathy and
Christian Science. To the last both the others are distinctly inferior,
for Christian Science will cure imaginary diseases, and they can not.
  The Devil's Dictionary

Physician: One upon whom we set our hopes when ill and our dogs
when well.
  Ibid

James Bryce, Viscount Bruce
Medicine is the only profession that labours incessantly to destroy
the reason for its own existence.
  New York, 1914

Anton Pavlovich Chekhov
Doctors are just the same as lawyers; the only difference is that
lawyers merely rob you, whereas doctors rob you and kill you, too.
  Ivanov

Marcus Tullius Cicero
Because all the sick do not recover, therefore medicine is no art.
  De Natura Deorum

J. Chalmers Da Costa
A fashionable surgeon like a pelican can be recognized by the size of his bill.
The Trials and Triumphs of the Surgeon

Samuel Goldwyn
Anbody who goes to see a psychiatrist ought to have his head examined.
Attributed

Hippocrates
Wherever the art of medicine is loved, there also is love of humanity.
Aphorisms

Oliver Wendell Holmes
I firmly believe that if the whole *materia medica*, as now used, could be sunk to the bottom of the sea, it would be all the better for mankind—and all the worse for the fishes.
Massachusetts Medical Society, 1860

Baron Gottfried Wilhelm von Leibnitz
I often say a great doctor kills more people than a great general.
Attributed

Leonardo da Vinci
Strive to preserve your health; and in this you will the better succeed in proportion as you keep clear of the physicians.
Notebooks

John Coakley Lettsom
When people's ill, they come to I,
I physics, bleeds, and sweats 'em;
Sometimes they live, sometimes they die.
What's that to I? I let's 'em.
On Dr Lettsom, by Himself

Molière [Jean-Baptiste Poquelin]
Nearly all men die of their medicines, not of their diseases.
Le malade imaginaire

Michel Eyquem de Montaigne
No doctor takes pleasure in the health even of his friends.
Essays

Napoleon I [Napoleon Bonaparte]
You medical people will have more lives to answer for in the other world than even we generals.
To Barry E. O'Meara, St Helena, 1817

Sir William Osler
The desire to take medicine is perhaps the greatest feature which distinguishes men from animals.
Science and Immortality

A physician who treats himself has a fool for a patient.
Sir William Osler: Aphorisms by William B. Bean

Ovid [Publius Ovidius Naso]
The art of medicine is generally a question of time.
Remedia Amoris

Medicine sometimes snatches away health, sometimes gives it.
Tristia

John Owen
God and the doctor we alike adore
But only when in danger, not before;
The danger o'er, both are alike requited,
God is forgotten, and the doctor slighted.
Epigrammata

Matthew Prior
Cured yesterday of my disease,
I died last night of my physician.
The Remedy Worse than the Disease

You tell your doctor that y' are ill,
And what does he do but write a bill?
Alma

Jean-Paul Sartre
Doctors, priests, magistrates, and officers know men as thoroughly
as if they had made them.
   Nausea

William Shakespeare
With the help of a surgeon, he might yet recover, and prove an ass.
   A Midsummer Night's Dream 5

George Bernard Shaw
The most tragic thing in the world is a sick doctor.
   The Doctor's Dilemma

Jonathan Swift
The best doctors in the world are Doctor Diet,
Doctor Quiet and Doctor Merryman.

Publilius Syrus
That sick man does badly who makes his physician his heir.
   Sententiae

Food & Gluttony

Kingsley Amis
Outside every fat man is an even fatter man trying to close in.
  One Fat Englishman

R(ichard) H(arris) Barham ["Thomas Ingoldsby"]
'Tis not her coldness, father,
That chills my labouring breast;
It's that confounded cucumber
I've eat and can't digest.
  The Ingoldsby Legends, 'The Confession'

Sir John Betjeman
Phone for the fish-knives, Norman,
  As Cook is a little unnerved.
  How to Get On in Society

The Bible
Let us eat and drink for tomorrow we shall die.
  Psalms 22

And when he had taken the five loaves and the two fishes, he looked
up to heaven, and blessed, and brake the loaves, and gave them to his
disciples to set before them; and the two fishes divided he among
them all. And they did all eat, and were filled. And they took up
twelve baskets full of the fragments, and of the fishes. And they that
did eat of the loaves were about five thousand men.
  Mark 6

Arnold Bennett
A man of sixty has spent twenty years in bed and over three years
eating.
  In *Bartlett's Unfamiliar Quotations*

Ambrose (Gwinett) Bierce
Eat: To perform successively (and successfully) the functions of mastication, humectation, and deglutition.
The Devil's Dictionary

Edible: good to eat, and wholesome to digest, as a worm to a toad, a toad to a snake, a snake to a pig, a pig to a man, and a man to a worm.
Ibid

Glutton: A person who escapes the evils of moderation by committing dyspepsia.
Ibid

Hospitality: the virtue which induces us to feed and lodge certain persons who are not in need of food and lodging.
Ibid

Sauce: the one infallible sign of civilization and enlightenment. A people with no sauces has one thousand vices; a people with one sauce has only nine hundred and ninety-nine.
Ibid

Rupert Chawner Brooke
Stands the Church clock at ten to three?
And is there honey still for tea.
The Old Vicarage, Grantchester

Robert Browning
So munch on, crunch on, take your muncheon
Breakfast, supper, dinner, luncheon!
The Pied Piper of Hamelin

Edmund Burke
And having looked to government for bread, on the very first scarcity they will turn and bite the hand that fed them.
Thoughts and Details on Scarcity

Robert Burns
The halesome parritch, chief of Scotia's food.
The Cottar's Saturday Night

Great chieftain o' the pudding-race.
  Address to a Haggis

Some hae meat and canna eat,
  And some wad eat that want it;
But we hae meat, and we can eat,
  And sae the Lord be thankit.
  The Selkirk Grace

George Gordon (Noel), 6th Lord Byron
  All human history attests
That happiness for man—the hungry sinner!—
Since Eve ate apples, much depends on dinner.
  Don Juan

Lewis Carroll [Charles Lutwidge Dodgson]
Jam tomorrow and jam yesterday—but never jam today.
  Through the Looking-Glass and What Alice Found There .

Cicero
One should eat to live, not live to eat.
  Rhetoricum

Cyril Connolly
Imprisoned in every fat man a thin one is wildly signalling to be let out.
  The Unquiet Grave

The one way to get thin is to re-establish a purpose in life.
  Ibid

Obesity is a mental state, a disease brought on by boredom and disappointment
  Ibid

Charles T. Copeland
To eat is human, to digest divine.

T(homas) S(tearns) Eliot
Should I, after tea and cakes and ices,

Have the strength to force the moment to its crisis?
The Love Song of J. Alfred Prufrock

Epicurus
We should look for someone to eat and drink with before looking for
something to eat and drink, for dining alone is leading the life of a
lion or wolf.
Aphorisms

Ludwig Andreas Feuerbach
Der Mensch is was er isst.
Man is what he eats.
Moleschott's *Lehre der Nahrungsmittel*, Preface

Benjamin Franklin
To lengthen thy life, lessen thy meals.
Poor Richard's Almanac 1733

Mahatma Gandhi (Mohandas Karamchand Gandhi)
I eat to live, to serve, and also, if it so happens, to enjoy, but I do not
eat for the sake of enjoyment.
Attributed

Hebrew Proverb
He that eats till he is sick must fast till he is well.

Dr Samuel Johnson
For a man seldom thinks with more earnestness of anything than he
does of his dinner.
Mrs Piozzi's *Anecdotes of Samuel Johnson*

Fran Lebowitz
Food is an important part of a balanced diet.
Metropolitan Life, "Food for Thought and Vice Versa'

Henry Sambrooke Leigh
If you wish to grow thinner, diminish your dinner,
    And take to light claret instead of pale ale;
Look down with an utter contempt upon butter,

And never touch bread till it's toasted—or stale.
  Carols of Cockayne

Marie Antoinette
Qu'ils mangent de la brioche.
Let them eat cake.
  Attributed

W(illiam) Somerset Maugham
At a dinner party one should eat wisely but not too well, and talk
well but not too wisely.
  A Writer's Notebook

George Meredith
Kissing don't last: cookery do!
  The Ordeal of Richard Feverel

A(lan) A(lexander) Milne
I do like a little bit of butter to my bread.
  When We Were Very Young

Molière [Jean-Baptiste Poquelin]
He makes his cook his merit, and the world visits his dinners and not
him.
  Le Misanthrope

Il faut manger pour vivre et non pas vivre pour manger.
One should eat to live, not live to eat.
  L'Avare

Ogden Nash
You two can be what you like, but since I am the big fromage in this
family, I prefer to think of myself as the Gorgon Zola.
  Medusa and the Mot Juste

Alexander Pope
Fame is at best an unperforming cheat;
But 'tis substantial happiness, to eat.
  Prologue for Mr D'Urfey's Last Play

François Rabelais
L'appetit vient en mangeant.
The appetite comes with eating.
  Gargantua

Harry Secombe
My advice if you insist on slimming: Eat as much a you like—just don't swallow it.
  The Daily Herald, 5 Oct. 1962

William Shakespeare
He hath eaten me out of house and home.
  King Henry IV, Part II 2

I am a great eater of beef and I believe that does harm to my wit.
  Twelfth Night 1

  He was a man
Of an unbounded stomach.
  King Henry VIII 4

George Bernard Shaw
There is no love sincerer than the love of food.
  Man and Superman

Sydney Smith
Madam, I have been looking for a person who disliked gravy all my life; let us swear eternal friendship.
  Lady Holland's *Memoir of the Rev. Sydney Smith*

I am convinced digestion is the great secret of life.
  Letter to Arthur Kinglake

Socrates
Bad men live that they may eat and drink, whereas good men eat and drink that they may live.
  Plutarch's *How Young Men Ought to hear Poems*

Jonathan Swift
Fingers were made before forks, and hands before knives.
  Polite Conversation

Drink & Abstinence

Alvan L. Bach
An alcoholic has been lightly defined as a man who drinks more than his own doctor.
  Journal of the American Medical Association, 1962

Pierre-Augustin Caron de Beaumarchais
Drinking when we are not thirsty and making love all year round, madam; that is all there is to distinguish us from other animals.
  The Marriage of Figaro

Thomas Becon
For when the wine is in, the wit is out.
  Catechism

The Bible
Wine is a mocker, strong drink is raging: and whosoever is deceived thereby is not wise.
  Proverbs 20

They reel to and fro, and stagger like a drunken man, and are at their wit's end.
  Psalms 107

Drink no longer water, but use a little wine for thy stomach's sake.
  I Timothy 5

Wine is as good as life to a man, if it be drunk moderately: what life is then to a man that is without wine? for it was made to make men glad.
  Ecclesiasticus 31

Ambrose (Gwinett) Bierce
Wine, madame, is God's next best gift to man.
  The Devil's Dictionary

Anthelme Brillat-Savarin
A meal without wine is like a day without sunshine.
The Physiology of Taste

Robert Burns
Freedom and whisky gang the gither!
The Author's Earnest Cry and Prayer

George Gordon (Noel), 6th Lord Byron
There's nought, no doubt, so much the spirit calms
  As rum and true religion.
Don Juan

Let us have wine and women, mirth and laughter,
Sermons and soda water the day after.
Ibid

Miguel de Cervantes (Saavedra)
I drink when I have occasion for it, and sometimes when I have not.
Don Quixote

Samuel Taylor Coleridge
Water, water, everywhere.
Nor any drop to drink.
The Ancient Mariner

T(homas) S(tearns) Eliot
I have measured out my life with coffee spoons.
The Love Song of J. Alfred Prufrock

Epictetus
He is a drunkard who takes more than three glasses.
Encheiridion

François de Salignac de la Mothe Fénélon
Some of the most dreadful mischiefs that afflict mankind proceed
from wine; it is the cause of disease, quarrels, sedition, idleness,
aversion to labour, and every species of domestic disorder.
Télémaque

Henry Fielding
I am as sober as a judge.
Don Quixote in England

F(rancis) Scott (Key) Fitzgerald
First you take a drink, then the drink takes a drink, then the drink takes you.
Ackroyd by Jules Feiffer

George Herbert
He that goes to bed thirsty rises healthy.
Jacula Rudentum

Drink not the third glasse,— which thou can'st not tame.
The Temple: The Church Porch

A(lfred) E(dward) Housman
And malt does more than Milton can
To justify God's ways to man.
Ale, man, ale's the stuff to drink
For fellows whom it hurts to think.
A Shropshire Lad

Washington Irving
They who drink beer will think beer.
The Sketch-book: Stratford

Thomas Jefferson
I wish to see this beverage [beer] become common instead of the whiskey which kills one third of our citizens, and ruins their families.
Letter, 1815

Jerome K(lapka) Jerome
We drink one another's health and spoil our own.
Idle Thoughts of an Idle Fellow

H(enry) L(ouis) Mencken
I've made it a rule never to drink by daylight and never to refuse a drink after dark.
New York Post, 1945

John Motley Morehead
It's a long time between drinks.
  Said when Governor of North Carolina

Ogden Nash
Candy
Is dandy
But liquor
Is quicker
  Hard Lines, 'Reflection on Ice-Breaking'

John Selden
'Tis not the drinking that is to be blamed, but the excess.
  Table Talk: Humility

William Shakespeare
I have very poor and unhappy brains for drinking: I could wish
courtesy would invent some other custom of entertainment.
  Othello 2

Good wine is a good familiar creature, if it be well used.
  Ibid

It provokes the desire, but it takes away the performance. Therefore
much drink may be said to be an equivocator with lechery.
  Macbeth 2

George Bernard Shaw
I'm only a beer teetotaller, not a champagne teetotaller.
  Candida

Sir J(ohn C(ollings) Squire
But I am not so think as you drunk I am.
  Ballade of Soporific Absorption

Horace Walpole, 4th Earl of Oxford
I have a partiality for drunkenness, though I never practised it: it is a
reality; but what is sobriety, only the absence of drunkenness?
  Letter, 1789

Work & Enterprise

Dean Acheson
A memorandum is written not to inform the reader but to protect the writer.

(Joseph) Hilaire (Pierre) Belloc
Lord Finchley tried to mend the Electric Light
Himself. It struck him dead: and serve him right!
It is the business of the wealthy man
To give employment to the artisan.
  Epigrams

Ambrose (Gwinett) Bierce
Corporation: an ingenious device for obtaining individual profit without individual responsibility.
  The Devil's Dictionary

Merchant: one engaged in a commercial pursuit. A commercial pursuit is one in which the thing pursued is a dollar.
  Ibid

Otto von Bismarck
To youth I have but three words of counsel—work, work, work.
  Sayings of Bismarck

George Gordon (Noel), 6th Lord Byron
Such hath it been—shall be—beneath the sun
The many still must labour for the one.
  The Corsair

Thomas Carlyle
A man willing to work, and unable to find work, is perhaps the saddest sight that fortune's inequality exhibits under the sun.
  Chartism

Blessed is he who has found his work; let him ask no other blessedness.
   Past and Present

Captains of industry.
   Ibid

Work is the grand cure of all the maladies and miseries that ever beset mankind.
   Rectorial address, Edinburgh, 1866

Philip Dormer Stanhope, 4th Earl of Chesterfield
Without some dissimulation no business can be carried on at all.
   Letters to His Son

Henry Clay
The call for free trade is as unavailing as the cry of a spoiled child for the moon. It never has existed; it never will exist.
   Senate speech, 1832

R(obin) G(eorge) Collingwood
Perfect freedom is reserved for the man who lives by his own work and in that work does what he wants to do.
   Speculum Mentis

Charles Caleb Colton
Of the professions it may be said that soldiers are becoming too popular, parsons too lazy, physicians too mercenary, and lawyers too powerful.
   Lacon

Calvin Coolidge
The business of America is business.
   Speech, 1925

Sir Noel (Pierce) Coward
Work is much more fun than fun.
   The Observer, 1963

Clarence Seward Darrow
With all their faults, trade unions have done more for humanity than

any other organization of men that ever existed.
  The Railroad Trainman

Charles Dickens
Here's the rule, for bargains: "Do other men, for they would do you."
That's the true business precept.
  Martin Chuzzlewit

W(illiam) E(dward) B(urghardt) Du Bois
The return from your work must be the satisfaction which that work
brings you and the world's need of that work. With this, life is
heaven, or as near heaven as you can get. Without this—with work
which you despise, which bores you, and which the world doest not
need—this life is hell.
  To His Newborn Great-Grandson

John Kenneth Galbraith
The salary of the chief executive of the large corporation is not a
market award for achievement. It is frequently in the nature of a
warm personal gesture by the individual to himself.
  Annals of an Abiding Liberal

Oliver Goldsmith
And honour sinks where commerce long prevails.
  The Traveller

Samuel Goldwyn
I don't want any yes-men around me. I want everybody to tell me the
truth even if it costs them their jobs.
  Attributed

Richard Long Harkness
What is a committee? A group of the unwilling, picked from the unfit,
to do the unnecessary.
  New York Herald Tribune, 1960

Sir A(lan) P(atrick) Herbert
This high official, all allow,
Is grossly overpaid.

There wasn't any Board; and now
There isn't any trade.
  On the President of the Board of Trade

David Hume
Avarice, the spur of industry.
  Essays: Of Civil Liberty

Jerome K(lapka) Jerome
I like work; it fascinates me. I can sit and look at it for hours. I love
to keep it by me: the idea of getting rid of it nearly breaks my heart.
  Three Men in a Boat

Dr Samuel Johnson
Trade could not be managed by those who manage it if it had much
difficulty.
  Letter to Mrs Hester Thrale

Abraham Lincoln
My father taught me to work; he did not teach me to love it.

Ogden Nash
I sit in an office at 244 Madison Avenue,
And say to myself You have a responsible job, havenue?
  Spring comes to Murray Hill

Sir William Osler
The effective, moving, vitalizing work of the world is done between
the ages of twenty-five and forty.
  Life of Sir William Osler by Harvey Cushing

My second fixed idea is the uselessness of men above sixty years of
age, and the incalculable benefit it would be…men stopped work at
this age.
  Ibid

Cyril Northcote Parkinson
Work expands so as to fill the time available for its completion.
  Parkinson's Law, The Pursuit of Progress

Laurence Johnston Peter

Most hierarchies were established by men, who now monopolize the upper levels, thus depriving women of their rightful share of opportunities to achieve incompetence.

The Peter Principle

An economist is an expert who will know tomorrow why the things he predicted yesterday didn't happen today.

Peter's Quotations

Franklin Delano Roosevelt

No business which depends for existing on paying less than living wages to its workers has any right to continue in this country.

Address, 1933

Theodore Roosevelt

No man needs sympathy because he has to work...Far and away the best prize that life offers is the chance to work hard at work worth doing.

Address, 1903

William Shakespeare

To business that we love we rise betime,
And go to 't with delight.

Antony and Cleopatra 4

Let me have no lying: it becomes none but tradesmen.

The Winter's Tale 4

Adam Smith

The real price of every thing, what every thing really costs to the man who wants to acquire it, is the toil and trouble of acquiring it.

The Wealth of Nations

People of the same trade seldom meet together, even for merriment and diversion, but the conversation ends in a conspiracy against the public, or in some contrivance to raise prices.

Ibid

Robert Louis Stevenson

Everyone lives by selling something.

Across the Plains

Studs (Louis) Terkel

Perhaps it is this spectre that most haunts working men and women: the planned obsolescence of people that is of a piece with the planned obsolescence of the things they make. Or sell.

Working

William Makepeace Thackeray

"No business before breakfast, Glum!" says the King. "Breakfast first, business next."

The Rose and the Ring

Virgil [Publius Vergilius Maro]

Labor omnia vincit.

Work conquers all.

Georgics

Voltaire [François Marie Arouet]

Work keeps us from three great evils, boredom, vice, and need.

Candide

Arthur Wellesley, 1st Duke of Wellington

My rule always was to do the business of the day in the day.

Stanhope's *Notes of Conversations with the Duke of Wellington*

Katherine Whitehorn

I yield to no one in my admiration for the office as a social centre, but it's no place to get any work done.

Sunday Best

Oscar (Fingall O'Flahertie Wills) Wilde

Work is the refuge of people who have nothing better to do.

The Soul of Man under Socialism

Idleness

James Albery
He slept beneath the moon,
He basked beneath the sun;
He lived a life of going-to-do,
And died with nothing done.
  Epitaph Written for Himself

Thomas Becon
Idleness, which is the well-spring and root of all vice.
  Early Works

The Bible
Woe to the idle shepherd that leaveth the flock.
  Habakkuk 11

Go to the ant, thou sluggard; consider her ways, and be wise.
  Proverbs 6

John Bodenham
Idleness is the canker of the mind.
  Belvedere

Robert Burton
Idleness is an appendix to nobility.
  Anatomy of Melancholy

Thomas Carlyle
The foul sluggard's comfort: "It will last my time."
  Count Cagliostro: Flight Last

Philip Dormer Stanhope, 4th Earl of Chesterfield
Idleness is only the refuge of weak minds.
  Letters to His Son

IDLENESS

Christina of Sweden
We grow older more through indolence, than through age.
  Maxims (1660–1680)

John Clarke
Ever sick of the slothful guise,
Loath to bed and loath to rise.
  Parœmiologia

Samuel Taylor Coleridge
As idle as a painted ship
Upon a painted sea.
  The Ancient Mariner

William Cowper
Absence of occupation is not rest,
A mind quite vacant is a mind distress'd.
  Retirement

William Henry Davies
What is this life if, full of care,
We have no time to stand and stare?
  Leisure

Ralph Waldo Emerson
That man is idle who can do something better.

George Farquhar
Says little, thinks less, and does nothing at all, faith!
  The Beaux' Stratagem

Thomas Fuller
Idlenss makes the wit rust.
  Gnomologia

John Kenneth Galbraith
Meetings are indispensable when you don't want to do anything.
  Ambassador's Journal

Horace [Quintus Horatius Flaccus]
Strenua inertia.
Masterly inactivity.
  Epistles

Nathiel Howe
To do nothing is the way to be nothing.
  A Chapter of Proverbs

Victor (Marie) Hugo
Nothing is more dangerous than discontinued labour; it is habit lost.
A habit easy to abandon, difficult to resume.
  Les Misérables

Jerome K(lapka) Jerome
It is impossible to enjoy idling thoroughly unless one has plenty of
work to do.
  The Idle Thoughts of an Idle Fellow

Dr Samuel Johnson
Perhaps man is the only being that can properly be called idle.
  The Idler

To do nothing is in every man's power.
  The Rambler

Franz Kafka
There are two cardinal sins from which others spring: impatience
and laziness.
  Franz Kafka by Max Brod

Rudyard Kipling
Kiddies and grown ups too-oo-oo,
If we haven't enough to do-oo-oo,
       We get the hump,
       Cameelious hump,
The lump that is black and blue!
  Just-So Stories: The Camel's Hump

Charles Lamb
I am sure that indolence—indefeasible indolence—is the true state of man, and business the invention of the old Teazer.
Letter to Wordsworth, 28 Sept. 1805

Michel Eyquem de Montaigne
I have ever loved to repose myself, whether sitting or lying, with my heels as high or higher than my head.
Essays

Friedrich Wilhelm Nietzsche
Idleness is the parent of all psychology.
Twilight of the Idols

Alexander Pope
She went from opera, park, assembly, play,
To morning walks, and prayers three times a day;
To part her time 'twixt reading and bohea,
To muse, and spill her solitary tea,
Or o'er cold coffee trifle with the spoon,
Count the slow clock, and dine exact at noon.
Epistle to Mrs. Teresa Blount

John Ray
An idle brain is the devil's workshop.
English Proverbs

Seneca
Nihilque tam certum est quam otii vitia negotio discuti.
Nothing is so certain as that the evils of idleness can be shaken off by hard work.
Epistulæ as Lucilium

William Shakespeare
If all the year were playing holidays,
To sport would be as tedious as to work.
King Henry IV, Part 1

George Bernard Shaw
The ghostliest of all unrealities, the non-working man.
The Irrational Knot

A man who has has no office to go to—I don't care who he is—is a trial
of which you can have no conception.
Ibid

Richard Steele
The insupportable labour of doing nothing.
Spectator

James Thomson
Their only labour was to kill time;
And labour dire it is, and weary woe.
Castle of Indolence

Martin Farquhar Tupper
It is well to lie fallow for a while.
Of Good in Things Evil: Of Recreation

George Turberville
Eschew the idle life,
  Flee, flee from doing nought:
For never was there idle brain
  But bred an idle thought.
The Lover to Cupid for Mercy

Artemus Ward [Charles Farrar Browne]
I am happiest when I am idle. I could live for months without
performing any kind of labour, and at the expiration of that time I
should feel fresh and vigorous enough to go right on in the same way
for numerous more months.
Natural History

R. T. Wombat
The lazy man gets round the sun
As quickly as the busy one
Quatrains

The Arts

Aristotle
Art is a higher type of knowledge than experience.
  Metaphysics

In part, art completes what nature cannot elaborate; and in part, it imitates nature.
  Physics

Charlie Chaplin [Sir Charles Spencer Chaplin]
There are more valid facts and details in works of art than there are in history books.
  My Autobiography

Victor Cousin
L'art pour l'art.
Art for art's sake.
  Sorbonne Lectures

T(homas) S(tearns) Eliot
No artist produces great art by a deliberate attempt to express his own personality.
  Essay: Four Elizabethan Dramatists

Henry Havelock Ellis
Every artist writes his own autobiography.
  The New Spirit

Ralph Waldo Emerson
Every genuine work of art has as much reason for being as the earth and the sun.
  Society and Solitude: Civilization

Art is a jealous mistress, and if a man have a genius for painting, poetry, music, architecture, or philosophy, he makes a bad husband

and an ill provider.
Conduct of Life: Wealth

Artists must be sacrificed to their art. Like bees, they must put their
lives into the sting they give.
Letters and Social Aims: Inspiration

E(dward) M(organ) Forster

Works of art, in my opinion, are the only objects in the material
universe to possess internal order, and that is why, though I don't
believe that only art matters, I do believe in Art for Art's sake.
Art for Art's Sake

Paul Gauguin

Many excellent cooks are spoiled by going into the arts.
Cournos' *Modern Plutarch*

Art is either a plagiarist or a revolutionist.
Pathos of Distance by James Huneker

Elbert Hubbard

Art is not a thing: it is a way.
Epigrams

James Gibbon Huneker

Great Art is an instant arrested in eternity.
Pathos of Distance

Henry James

Art is nothing more than the shadow of humanity.
Lectures: University in Arts

John Keats

The excellence of every art is its intensity, capable of making all
disagreeables evaporate, from their being in close relationship with
beauty and truth.
Letter to his brothers, 1817

So I do believe...that works of genius are the first things in this world.
Ibid 1818

Rudyard Kipling
But the Devil whoops, as he whooped of old:
  "It's clever, but is it Art?"
  The Conundrum of the Workshops

H(enry) L(ouis) Mencken
The great artists of the world are never Puritans, and seldom even ordinarily respectable.
  Prejudices

George Augustus Moore
Art must be parochial in the beginning to be cosmopolitan in the end.
  Hail and Farewell

George Jean Nathan
Great art is as irrational as great music. It is mad with its own loveliness.
  House of Satan

Art is a reaching out into the uglinesss of the world for vagrant beauty and the imprisonment of it in a tangible dream.
  Critic and the Drama

Dorothy (Rothschild) Parker
Authors and actors and artists and such
Never know nothing and never know much…
Playwrights and poets and such horses' necks
Start off from anywhere, end up at sex.
  Bohemia

Edgar Allan Poe
Were I called upon to define, very briefly, the term "art," I should call it "the reproduction of what the senses perceive in nature through the veil of the soul."
  Marginalia

Quintillian [Marcus Fabius Quintilianus]
The height of art is to conceal art.
  De institutione oratoria

John Ruskin

All great art is the work of the whole living creature, body and soul, and—chiefly of the soul.

The Stones of Venice

No one can explain how the notes of a Mozart melody, or the folds of a piece of Titian's drapery, produce their essential effects. If you do not feel it, no one can by reasoning make you feel it.

Ibid

Life without industry is guilt, industry without art is brutality.

Lectures on Art

George Bernard Shaw

The true artist will let his wife starve, his children go barefoot, his mother drudge for his living at seventy, sooner than work at anything but his art.

Man and Superman

Count Leo (Nikolaevich) Tolstoy

Art is not a handicraft, it is a transmission of feeling the artist has experienced.

What is Art?

James (Abbott) McNeill Whistler

Art happens—no hovel is safe from it, no Prince may depend on it, the vastest intelligence cannot bring it about.

"Ten O'Clock."

Oscar (Fingall O'Flahertie Wills) Wilde

The final revelation is that Lying, the telling of beautiful untrue things, is the proper aim of Art.

Intentions: The Decay of Lying

The secret of life is in art.

The English Renaissance

Art should never try to be popular.

The Soul of Man under Socialism

Music

Joseph Addison
Music, the greatest good that mortals know,
And all of heaven we have below.
  Song for St Cecilia's Day

Jane Austen
I consider music as a very innocent diversion, and perfectly
compatible with the profession of a clergyman.
  Pride and Prejudice

Sir Thomas Beecham
Music first and last should sound well, should allure and enchant the
ear. Never mind the inner significance.
  Atkins' and Newman's *Beecham Stories*

The function of music is to release us from the tyranny of conscious
thought.
  Ibid

A distinguished British historian…declares that solo singing is favour-
ed in an aristocratic society and communal or choral in a democratic.
  A Mingled Chime

Jazz! Bah—nothing but the debasement of noble brass instruments
by blowing them into mutes, hats, caps, nooks, crannies, holes and
corners!
  Brymer's *From Where I Sit*

Sir Max Beerbohm
"I don't," she added, "know anything about music, really. But I
know what I like."
  Zuleika Dobson

The Bible
O sing unto the Lord a new song: sing unto the Lord, all the earth.
  Psalms 96

Ambrose (Gwinett) Bierce

Opera: a play representing life in another world, whose inhabitants have no speech but song, no motions but gestures and no postures but attitudes.

The Devil's Dictionary

Piano: a parlor utensil for subduing the impenitent visitor. It is operated by depressing the keys of the machine and the spirits of the audience.

Ibid

William Cobbett

Dancing is at once rational and healthful.

Advice to Young Men

Samuel Taylor Coleridge

Swans sing before they die—'twere no bad thing
Should certain persons die before they sing.

Epigram on a Volunteer Singer

William Congreve

Music alone with sudden charms can bind
The wandering sense, and calm the troubled mind.

Hymn to Harmony

Music has charms to soothe a savage breast.

The Mourning Bride

Sir Noel (Pierce) Coward

Extraordinary how potent cheap music is.

Private Lives

Aldous (Leonard) Huxley

After silence, that which comes nearest to expressing the inexpressible is music.

In Time

Gioacchino Antonio Rossini

Beethoven is the greatest composer—but Mozart is the only one.

Attributed

MUSIC

William Shakespeare
I am never merry when I hear sweet music.
  The Merchant of Venice 1

The man that hath no music in himself,
Nor is not moved with concord of sweet sounds,
Is fit for treasons, stratagems and spoils...
Let no such man be trusted.
  Ibid 5

If music be the food of love, play on.
  Twelfth Night 1

George Bernard Shaw
At every one of those concerts in England you will find rows of
weary people who are there, not because they really like classical
music, but because they think they ought to like it.
  Man and Superman

Percy Bysshe Shelley
Music, when soft voices die,
Vibrates in the memory.
  To —: Music When Soft Voices

Artemus Ward [Charles Farrar Browne]
I can't sing. As a singist I am not a success. I am saddest when I
sing. So are those who hear me. They are sadder even than I am.
  Artemus Ward, His Travels

Edith Wharton
An unalterable and unquestioned law of the musical world required
that the German text of French operas sung by Swedish artists
should be translated into Italian for the clearer understanding of
English-speaking audiences.
  The Age of Innocence

Painting & Sculpture

Sir Thomas Browne
I can look for a whole day with delight upon a handsome picture, though it be but of an horse.
   Religio Medici

Robert Browning
Your business is to paint the souls of men.
   Fra Lippo Lippi

Works done least rapidly, Art most cherishes.
   Old Pictures in Florence

That's my last Duchess painted on the wall
Looking as if she were alive.
   My Last Duchess

Sir Edward Coley Burne-Jones
I mean by a picture a beautiful, romantic dream of something that never was, never will be.
   Letter

Miguel de Cervantes (Saavedra)
Good painters imitate nature, bad ones regurgitate it.
   El Licenciado Vidriera

Oliver Cromwell
Mr Lely, I desire you would use all your skill to paint my picture freely like me, and not flatter me at all; but remark all these roughnesses, pimples, and everything as you see me, otherwise I will never pay a farthing for it.
   Attributed

Charles Dickens
There are only two styles of portrait painting; the serious and the smirk.
   Nicholas Nickleby

Oliver Goldsmith
When they talk'd of their Raphaels, Correggios, and stuff,
He shifted his trumpet, and only took snuff.
  Retaliation

William Hazlitt
Landscape painting is the obvious resource of misanthropy.
  Criticisms on Art

Indifferent pictures, like dull people, must absolutely be moral.
  Ibid

Dr Samuel Johnson
I had rather see the portrait of a dog that I know than all the allegorical paintings…in the world.
  Boswell's *Life of Johnson*

Henry Wadsworth Longfellow
Sculpture is more divine, and more like Nature,
That fashions all her works in high relief,
And that is sculpture. This vast ball, the Earth,
Was moulded out of clay, and baked in fire;
Men, women, and all animals that breathe
Are statues and not paintings.
  Michael Angelo

H(enry) H(art) Milman
And the cold marble leapt into life a god.
  The Belvedere Apollo

"Grandma" (Anna Mary) Moses
A primitive artist is an amateur whose work sells.

Alexander Pope
Then marble, soften'd into life, grew warm.
  Imitations of Horace: Epistles

John Ruskin
No picture can be good which deceives by its imitation, for the very reason that nothing can be beautiful which is not true.
  Modern Painters

They are good furniture pictures, unworthy of praise, and undeserving of blame.
Ibid

James Thomson
So stands the statue [the Venus de Medici] that enchants the world.
The Seasons: Summer

Ivan Sergeyevich Turgenev
A picture shows me at a glance what it takes dozen of pages of a book to expound.
Fathers and Sons

C(harles) D(udley) Warner
A great artist can paint a great picture on a small canvas.
Washington Irving

James Abbott McNeill Whistler
A life passed among pictures makes not a painter—else the policeman in the National Gallery might assert himself. As well assert that he who lives in a library must needs be a poet.
The Gentle Art of Making Enemies

Poetry

Matthew Arnold

Poetry is simply the most beautiful, impressive and widely effective mode of saying things, and hence its importance.

Essays in Criticism: Heinrich Heine

Not deep the Poet sees, but wide.

Resignation

Thomas Beer

I agree with one of your reputable critics that a taste for drawing-rooms has spoiled more poets than ever did a taste for gutters.

The Mauve Decade

Robert Browning

Would you have your songs endure?
Build on the human heart!

Sordello

Robert Burns

Hail, Poesie! thou nymph reserv'd!
In chase o' thee, what crowds hae swerv'd
Frae Common Sense, or sunk ennerv'd
  'Mang heaps o' clavers.

Sketch

Robert Burton

All poets are mad.

Anatomy of Melancholy.

Samuel Butler

For rhyme the rudder is of verses,
With which, like ships, they steer their courses.

Hudibras

Marcus Tullius Cicero

Adhuc neminem cognovi poetam, qui sibi non optimus videretur.
I have never yet known a poet who did not think himself the best.
   Tusculanarum Disputationum

Samuel Taylor Coleridge

No man was ever yet a great poet, without being at the same time a
profound philosopher.
   Biographia Literaria

That willing suspension of disbelief for the moment, which
constitutes poetic faith.
   Ibid

Not the poem which we have read, but that to which we return, with
the greatest pleasure, possesses the genuine power, and claims the
name of essential poetry.
   Lectures on Shakespeare and Milton

I wish our clever young poets would remember my homely
definitions of prose and poetry; that is, prose = words in their best
order; poetry = the best words in the best order.
   Table Talk

Charles Caleb Colton

Subtract from many modern poets all that may be found in
Shakespeare, and trash will remain.
   Lacon

William Cowper

There is a pleasure in poetic pains
Which only poets know.
   The Task II: The Timepiece

Isaac D'Israeli

A poet is the painter of the soul.
   Literary Characters of Men of Genius

John Donne

I am two fooles, I know,

For loving, and for saying so
In whining Poetry.
   The Triple Foole

Ralph Waldo Emerson
Homer's words are as costly and admirable to Homer as
Agamemnon's victories are to Agamemnon.
   Essays: Second Series

Poets often have nothing poetical about them except their verses.
   Conduct of Life: Behaviour

James Elroy Flecker
The poet's business is not to save the soul of man but to make it
worth saving.
   Untermeyer's *Modern British Poetry*

Johann Wolfgang von Goethe
Neuere Poeten thun viel Wasser in die Tinte.
Modern poets mix too much water with their ink.
   Sprüche in Prosa

(Sir) Anthony Hope (Hawkins)
I wish you would read a little poetry sometimes. Your ignorance
cramps my conversation.
   The Dolly Dialogues

Horace [Quintus Horatius Flaccus]
Genus irritabile vatum.
The touchy race of poets.
   Epistles

Incomposito pede currere versus.
His verses run with a halting foot.
   Satires

The man is mad, or else he's writing verses.
   Ibid

Poets, the first instructors of mankind.
   Ars Poetica

Ben(jamin) Jonson
A good poet's made as well as born.
To the Memory of Shakespeare

(Alfred) Joyce Kilmer
I think that I shall never see
A poem lovely as a tree.
Trees

Poems are made by fools like me,
But only God can make a tree.
Ibid

The Koran
Those who err follow the poets.
Ch. 26

Thomas Babington Macaulay, 1st Baron Macaulay
Perhaps no person can be a poet, or even can enjoy poetry, without a certain unsoundness of mind.
Essays: On Milton

H(enry) L(ouis) Mencken
Nine-tenths of the best poetry of the world has been written by poets less than thirty years old; a great deal more than half of it has been written by poets under twenty-five.
Prejudices

Plato
Poets utter great and wise things which they do not themselves understand.
The Republic

Alexander Pope
It stands on record, that in Richard's times
A man was hang'd for very honest rhymes.
Imitations of Horace: Satires

William Shakespeare
The lunatic, the lover and the poet

Are of imagination all compact.
  A Midsummer Night's Dream 5

Tear him for his bad verses, tear him for his bad verses.
  Julius Caesar 3

This is the very false gallop of verses.
  As you Like It 3

Percy Bysshe Shelley
Poetry is the record of the best and happiest moments of the happiest
and best minds.
  A Defence of Poetry

Alfred, Lord Tennyson
The passionate heart of the poet is whirl'd
        into folly and vice.
  Maud

Dylan Thomas
These poems, with all their crudities, doubts, and confusions, are
written for the love of Man and in praise of God, and I'd be a damn'
fool if they weren't.
  Collected Poems, Note

Franz Woepcke
I have seized life by the the poetic side.
  Journals of Ralph Waldo Emerson, 1868

William Wordsworth
We poets in our youth begin in gladness;
But thereof comes in the end despondency and madness.
  The Leech-Gatherer; or Resolution and Independence

Poetry is the spontaneous overflow of powerful feelings: it takes its
origin from emotion recollected in tranquility.
  Lyrical Ballads, Preface

Books & Reading

(Amos) Bronson Alcott
One must be a wise reader to quote wisely and well.
  Table Talk: Quotation

Jane Austen
I think I may boast myself to be, with all possible vanity, the most unlearned and uninformed female who ever dared to be an authoress.
  Letter, 1815

"And what are you reading, Miss ——?" "Oh! it is only a novel!" replies the young lady; while she lays down her book with affected indifference, or momentary shame.
  Northanger Abbey

Francis Bacon
Some books are to be tasted, others to be swallowed, and some few to be chewed and digested.
  Essays: Of Studies

(Joseph) Hilaire (Pierre) Belloc
When I am dead, I hope it may be said
"His sins were scarlet, but his books were read."
  On His Books

The Bible
Of making many books there is no end; and much study is a weariness of the flesh.
  Ecclesiastes 12

Ambrose (Gwinett) Bierce
Novel: a short story padded.
  The Devil's Dictionary

The first three essentials of the literary art are imagination, imagination and imagination.
Ibid

Charlotte Brontë
Novelists should never allow themselves to weary of the study of real life.
The Professor

Robert Burton
Hence it is clear how much more cruel the pen is than the sword.
Anatomy of Melancholy

George Gordon (Noel) Byron, 6th Lord Byron
'Tis pleasant, sure, to see one's name in print;
A book's a book, although there's nothing in 't.
English Bards and Scotch Reviewers

If I could always read, I should never feel the want of society.
Journal

Thomas Carlyle
My books are friends that never fail me.
Letter, 1817

A well-written Life is amost as rare as a well-spent one.
Critical and Miscellaneous Essays

Lewis Carroll [Charles Lutwidge Dodgson]
"What is the use of a book," thought Alice, "without pictures or conversations?"
Alice's Adventures in Wonderland

G(ilbert K(eith) Chesterton
There is a great deal of difference between the eager man who wants to read a book, and the tired man who wants a book to read.
Charles Dickens

William Cowper
Thousands...
Kiss the book's outside who ne'er look within.
Expostulation

Benjamin Disraeli, 1st Earl of Beaconsfield
An author who speaks about his own books is almost as bad as a mother who talks about her own children.
Banquet, 1873

When I want to read a novel I write one.
Moneypenny and Buckle's *Life of Disraeli*

Isaac D'Israeli
There is an art of reading, as well as an art of thinking, and an art of writing.
The Literary Character

T(homas) S(tearns) Eliot
Many are engaged in writing books and printing them
Many desire to see their names in print,
Many read nothing but the race reports.
The Rock

Ralph Waldo Emerson
Never read any book that is not a year old.
Society and Solitude: Books

Edward Gibbon
My early and invincible love of reading…I would not exchange for the treasures of India.
Memoirs

William Henry, Duke of Gloucester
Another damned, thick, square book! Always scribble, scribble, scribble. Eh! Mr Gibbon?
Attributed

Heinrich Heine
Wherever they burn books they will also, in the end, burn human beings.
Almansor: A Tragedy

Ernest Hemingway
All modern American literature comes from one book by Mark

Twain called Huckleberry Finn.
  Green Hills of Africa

Aldous (Leonard) Huxley
The proper study of mankind is books.
  Chrome Yellow

William Ralph Inge
Literature flourishes best when it is half a trade and half an art.
  The Victorian Age

Henry James
It takes a great deal of history to produce a little literature.
  Life of Nathaniel Hawthorne

Dr Samuel Johnson
What is written without effort is in general read without pleasure.
  Johnsonian Miscellanies

A man ought to read just as inclination leads him; for what he reads
as a task will do him little good.
  Boswell's *Life of Johnson*

[When asked if he had read a new book through] No, Sir, do *you*
read books *through*?
  Ibid

A man will turn over half a library to make one book.
  Ibid

Helen (Adams) Keller
Literature is my Utopia. Here I am not disfranchised. No barrier of
the senses shuts me out from the sweet, gracious discourse of my
book friends. They talk to me without embarrassment or
awkwardness.
  The Story of My Life

Georg Christoph Lichtenberg
There can hardly be a stranger commodity in the world than books.
Printed by people who don't understand them; sold by people who

don't understand them; bound, criticized and read by people who don't understand them, and now even written by people who don't understand them.
A Doctrine of Scattered Occasions

Samuel Lover
When once the itch of literature comes over a man, nothing can cure it but the scratching of a pen.
Handy Andy

Martin Luther
The multitude of books is a great evil.
Table-Talk

Michel Eyquem de Montaigne
All the world knows me in my book, and my book in me.
Essays

John Morley, 1st Viscount Morley of Blackburn
Literature, the most seductive, the most deceiving, the most dangerous of professions.
Burke

Dorothy (Rothschild) Parker
This is not a novel to be tossed aside lightly. It should be thrown with great force.

Will(iam Penn Adair) Rogers
When you put down the good things you ought to have done, and leave out the bad ones you did do—that's memoirs.
The Autobiography of Will Rogers

John Ruskin
All books are divisible into two classes: the books of the hour, and the books of all time.
Seasame and Lilies

If a book is worth reading, it is worth buying.
Ibid

William Shakespeare

He hath never fed of the dainties that are bred in a book; he hath not
eat paper, as it were; he hath not drunk ink.
  Love's Labour's Lost 1

Knowing I loved my books, he furnish'd me
From mine own library with volumes that
I prize above my dukedom.
  The Tempest 1

(Lloyd) Logan Pearsall Smith

A bestseller is the gilded tomb of a mediocre talent.
  Afterthoughts: Art and Letters

People say that life is the thing, but I prefer reading.
  Ibid: Myself

Sydney Smith

No furniture so charming as books.
  Lady Holland's *Memoirs of the Rev. Sydney Smith*

Sir Richard Steele

Reading is to the mind what exercise is to the body.
  The Tatler

Robert Louis Stevenson

Books are good enough in their own way, but they are a mighty
bloodless substitute for life.
  Virginibus Puerisque: An Apology for Idlers

Jonathan Swift

Satire is a sort of glass, wherein beholders do generally discover
everybody's face but their own.
  The Battle of the Books

William Makepeace Thackeray

There are a thousand thoughts lying within a man that he does not
know till he takes up the pen to write.
  The History of Henry Esmond

Thomas à Kempis

Verily, when the day of judgment comes, we shall not be asked what

we have read, but what we have done.
De Imitatione Christi

Henry David Thoreau
How many a man has dated a new era in his life from the reading of
a book.
Walden

Martin Farquhar Tupper
A good book is the best of friends, the same today and for ever.
Proverbial Philosophy: Of Reading

Mark Twain [Samuel Langhorne Clemens]
A classic is something that everybody wants to have read and
nobody wants to read.
Speeches: The Disappearance of Literature

John Wesley
Beware you be not swallowed up in books! An ounce of love is
worth a pound of knowledge.
Southey's *Life of Wesley*

Oscar (Fingall O'Flahertie Wills) Wilde
There is no such thing as a moral or an immoral book. Books are
well written or badly written. That is all.
The Picture of Dorian Gray

You should study the Peerage, Gerald. It is the one book a young
man about town should know thoroughly, and it is the best thing in
fiction the English have done.
A Woman of No Importance

I never travel without my diary. One should always have something
sensational to read in the train.
The Importance of Being Earnest

William Wordsworth
Every great and original writer, in proportion as he is great and
original, must himself create the taste by which he is to be relished.
Letter

Film & Theatre

Robert Benchley
There's less in this than meets the eye.
[After viewing an art film.]
   Halliwells' *Filmgoer's and Video Viewer's Companion*

Marlon Brando
An actor's a guy who if you ain't talkin' about him, ain't listening.
   The Observer, 1956

Fanny Burney [Frances, Madame d'Arblay]
"Do you come to the play without knowing what it is?"
"Oh, yes, sir, yes, very frequently. I have not time to read playbills.
One merely comes to meet one's friends, and show that one's alive."
   Evelina

Oliver Goldsmith
On the stage he was natural, simple, affecting;
'Twas only that when he was off he was acting.
   Retaliation

Moss Hart
One begins with two people on a stage and one of them had better
say something pretty damn quick!
   Contemporary Dramatists, 1977

Katharine Hepburn
Acting's just waiting for a custard pie. That's all.

Sir Alfred (Joseph) Hitchcock
The length of a film should be directly related to the endurance of
the human bladder.
   The Observer, 1960

If I made Cinderella, the audience would be looking out for a body in the coach.

Auguste (Marie Louis Nicolas) Lumière
Young man, you may be grateful that my invention is not for sale, for it would undoubtedly ruin you. It can be exploited for a certain time as a scientific curiosity, but apart from that it has no commercial value whatsoever.
  Said 1895

George Augustus Moore
Acting is therefore the lowest of the arts, if it is an art at all.
  Mummer-Worship

Francis Quarles
Judge not the play before the play is done:
  Epigram: Respice Finem

William Shakespeare
The play, I remember, pleased not the million; 'twas caviare to the general.
  Hamlet 2

The play's the thing
Wherein I'll catch the conscience of the king.
  Ibid

Speak the speech, I pray you, as I pronounced it to you, trippingly on the tongue: but if you mouth it, as many of your players do, I had as lief the town-crier spoke my lines. Nor do not saw the air too much with your hand, thus, but use all gently.
  Ibid

Suit the action to the word, the word to the action; with this special observance, that you o'erstep not the modesty of nature.
  Ibid

The purpose of playing, whose end, both at the first and now, was and is, to hold, as 'twere, the mirror up to nature.
  Ibid

Exit, pursued by a bear.
   The Winter's Tale 3, stage direction

Spencer Tracy
Acting in not an important job in the scheme of things. Plumbing is.
I'm too tired and old and rich for all this. so let's do the scene.
[To a director with "artistic" pretensions.]
   Halliwells' *Filmgoer's and Video Viewer's Companion*

Billy Wilder
Johnny, keep it out of focus. I want to win the foreign picture award.
[To his cinematographer]
   Halliwells' *Filmgoer's and Video Viewer's Companion*

Mass Media

Jean Anouilh
Have you noticed that life, real honest to goodness life, with
murders, and catastrophes and fabulous inheritances, happens almost
exclusively in newspapers?
The Rehearsal

W(ystan) H(ugh) Auden
What the mass media offer is not popular art, but entertainment
which is intended to be consumed like food, forgotten, and replaced
by a new dish.
The Dyer's Hand: The Poet and the City

(Enoch) Arnold Bennett
Journalists say a thing that they know isn't true in the hope that if
they keep on saying it long enough it will be true.
The Title

(Mark) James (Walter) Cameron
The press can only be a mirror—albeit a distorting mirror, according
to its politics or the smallness of its purpose—but it rarely lies
because it dare not.
The Listener, 1979

Quentin Crisp
If any reader of this book is in the grip of some habit of which he is
deeply ashamed, I advise him not to give way to it in secret but to do
it on television…People will cross the road at the risk of losing their
own lives in order to say "We saw you on the telly."
How to Become a Virgin

Charles Anderson Dana
When a dog bites a man that is not news, but when a man bites a dog
that is news.
'What is News?', *New York Sun,* 1882

T(homas) S(tearns) Eliot
[TV] is a medium of entertainment which permits millions of people to listen to the same joke at the same time, and yet remain lonesome.
New York Post, 1963

David (Parradine) Frost
Television is an invention that permits you to be entertained in your living room by people you wouldn't have in your home.
David Frost Revue, CBS TV, 1971

Samuel Goldwyn
Why should people go out and pay money to see bad films when they can stay at home and see bad television for nothing?
The Observer, 1956

Richard Ingrams
Children watch too much television not only because indolent parents allow them to, but because the standard of most programmes is pitched at their level.
The Observer

Thomas Jefferson
Where the press is free and every man able to read, all is safe.
Writings, Vol. XIV

"Junius" [?Sir Philip Francis]
The liberty of the press is the Palladium of all the civil, political, and religious rights of an Englishman.
Letters, Dedication

Louis Kronenberger
It is the gossip columnist's business to write about what is none of his business.
The Cart and the Horse

(Herbert) Marshall McLuhan
The medium is the message.
Understanding Media

Advertising is the greatest art form of the twentieth century.
  Advertising Age

Norman Mailer
Once a newspaper touches a story, the facts are lost forever, even to the protagonists.
  The Presidential Papers

Groucho (Julius Henry) Marx
I find television very educational. Every time someone switches it on I go into another room and read a good book.
  The Groucho Papers

George Mason
The freedom of the press is one of the great bulwarks of liberty, and can never be restrained but by despotic governments.
  Virginia Bill of Rights, 1776

Sir Yehudi Menuhin
Whenever I see a newspaper, I think of the poor trees. As trees they provide beauty, shade and shelter, but as paper all they provide is rubbish.
  Said 1970

Arthur Miller
A good newspaper is a nation talking to itself.
  The Observer, 1961

Alfred Charles William Harmsworth, Viscount Northcliffe
A profession [journalism] whose business it is to explain to others what it personally does not understand.

Adolph Simon Ochs
All the news that's fit to print.
  [Motto of the New York Times.]

John (Henry) O'Hara
Hot lead can be almost as effective coming from a linotype as from a firearm.
  The Portable F. Scott Fitzgerald, Introduction

Theodore Roosevelt
The men with the muck-rake are often indispensable to the well-being of society, but only if they know when to stop raking the muck.
  Address, 1906

C(harles) P(restwich) Scott
Television? The word is half Latin and half Greek. No good can come of it.
  Attributed

Richard Brinsley Sheridan
The newspapers! Sir, they are the most villainous—licentious—abominable—infernal—Not that I ever read them—no—I make it a rule never to look into a newspaper.
  The Critic

Susan Sontag
Reality has come to seem more and more like what we are shown by cameras.
  'Photography Unlimited', *New York Review of Books,* 1977

Voltaire [François Marie Arouet]
In the case of news, we should always wait for the sacrament of confirmation.

Barbara Ward
The modern world is not given to uncritical admiration. It expects its idols to have feet of clay, and can be reasonably sure that press and camera will report their exact dimensions.
  Saturday Review, 1961

Oscar (Fingall O'Flahertie Wills) Wilde
As for modern journalism, it is not my business to defend it. It justifies its own existence by the great Darwinian principle of the survival of the vulgarist.
  Intentions: The Critic as Artist

There is much to be said in favour of modern journalism. By giving

us the opinions of the uneducated, it keeps us in touch with the ignorance of the community.
Ibid

Billy Wilder
Television is...a twenty-one inch person. I'm delighted with it, because it used to be that films were the lowest form of art. Now we've got something to look down on.
  Halliwell's *Filmgoer's Book of Quotations*

Foolishness & Wisdom

Phineas Taylor Barnum
You can fool some of the people all the time, and all of the people some of the time, but you can't fool all of the people all the time.
   Attributed

The Bible
Wisdom is the principal thing; therefore get wisdom: and with all thy getting get understanding.
   Proverbs 4

Even a fool, when he holdeth his peace, is counted wise: and he that shutteth his lips is esteemed a man of understanding.
   Ibid 17

It is an honour for a man to cease from strife: but every fool will be meddling.
   Ibid 20

Answer not a fool according to his folly, lest thou also be like unto him. Answer a fool according to his folly, lest he be wise in his own conceit.
   Ibid 26

For in much wisdom is much grief: and he that increaseth knowledge increaseth sorrow.
   Ecclesiastes 1

The heart of the wise is in the house of mourning: but the heart of fools is in the house of mirth. It is better to hear the rebuke of the wise, than for a man to hear the song of fools.
   Ibid 7

For ye suffer fools gladly, seeing ye yourselves are wise.
   2 Corinthians 11

William Blake
A fool sees not the same tree that a wise man sees.
  Marriage of Heaven and Hell: Proverbs of Hell

Nicolas Boileau-Despréaux
A fool always finds a greater fool to admire him.
  L'Art poétique

Miguel de Cervantes (Saavedra)
He's a muddled fool, full of lucid intervals.
  Don Quixote

Charles Caleb Colton
The follies of the fool are known to the world, but are hidden from
himself; the follies of the wise are known to himself, but hidden
from the world.
  Lacon

Confucius
For one word a man is often deemed to be wise, and for one word he
is often deemed to be foolish. We should be careful indeed what we
say.
  Analects

William Cowper
How much a dunce that has been sent to roam
Excels a dunce that has been kept at home.
  The Progress of Error

Knowledge is proud that he has learn'd so much;
Wisdom is humble that he knows no more.
  The Task: The Winter Walk at Noon

Albert Einstein
Before God we are all equally wise—equally foolish.
  Address at the Sorbonne

Epicharmus
The wise man must be wise before, not after, the event.
  Fabulæ Incertæ

Benjamin Franklin
Experience keeps a dear school, but fools will learn in no other.
Poor Richard's Almanack 1743

It is ill manners to silence a fool, and cruelty to let him go on.
Ibid 1754

The first degree of folly is to conceit one's self wise; the second to profess it; the third to despise counsel.
Ibid

Baltasar Gracián
Self-reflection is the school of wisdom.
The Art of Worldly Wisdom

Thomas Gray
Where ignorance is bliss,
'Tis folly to be wise.
Ode on a Distant Prospect of Eton College

Henry IV
The wisest fool in Christendom. [James VI of Scotland and I of England.]
Attributed

Thomas Hobbes
For words are wise men's counters, they do but reckon by them; but they are the money of fools.
Leviathan

Thomas Henry Huxley
The only medicine for suffering, crime, and all the other woes of mankind, is wisdom.
Science and Education

Ben(jamin) Jonson
To be a fool born is a disease incurable.
Volpone

Rudyard Kipling
Take my word for it, the silliest woman can manage a clever man;

but it needs a very clever woman to manage a fool.
Three and—an Extra

Abraham Lincoln

You can fool some of the people all of the time, and all of the people some of the time, but you cannot fool all of the people all the time.
Attributed, 1856

Better to remain silent and be thought a fool than to speak out and remove all doubt.
Attributed

Lady Mary Wortley Montagu

I enjoy vast delight in the folly of mankind; and, God be praised, that is an inexhaustible source of entertainment.
Letter, 1725

Edgar Allan Poe

I have great faith in fools:—self-confidence my friends will call it.
Marginalia

Alexander Pope

Pride, the never-failing vice of fools.
Essay on Criticism

For fools rush in where angels fear to tread.
Ibid

No creature smarts so little as a fool.
Epistle to Dr Arbuthnot

Sir Walter Raleigh

Tell wisdom she entangles
Herself in overwiseness.
The Lie

Allan Ramsay

For when I dinna clearly see,
I always own I dinna ken,
And that's the way with wisest men.
Eclogue

FOOLISHNESS & WISDOM

Theodore Roosevelt
Nine-tenths of wisdom is being wise in time.
  Speech, 14 June 1917

William Shakespeare
Lord, what fools these mortals be!
  A Midsummer Night's Dream 3

I had rather have a fool to make me merry than experience to make
me sad.
  As You Like It 4

The fool doth think he is wise, but the wise man knows himself to be
a fool.
  Ibid 5

He uses his folly like a stalking-horse and under the presentation of
that he shoots his wit.
  Ibid

William Shenstone
A fool and his words are soon parted; a man of genius and his money.
  Essays on Men and Manners: On Reserve

Charles Hadden Spurgeon
The doorstep to the temple of wisdom is a knowledge of our own
ignorance.
  Gleanings among the Sheaves: The First Lesson

Laurence Sterne
Sciences may be learned by rote, but Wisdom not.
  Tristram Shandy

Alfred, Lord Tennyson
Knowledge comes, but wisdom lingers.
  Locksley Hall

Thomas Tusser
A fool and his money be soon at debate.
  Five Hundred Points of Good Husbandry

Samuel Warren
There is probably no man living, though ever so great a fool, that cannot do something or other well.
Ten Thousand a Year

Oscar (Fingall O'Flahertie Wills) Wilde
There is no sin except stupidity.
Intentions: The Critic as Artist

Teachers, Scholars & Critics

Henry (Brooks) Adams
A teacher affects eternity; he can never tell where his influence stops.
   The Education of Henry Adams

Anonymous Critic
Mr Dickens writes too often and too fast…If he persists much longer in this course, it requires not gift of prophecy to foretell his fate—he has risen like a rocket, and he will come down like a stick.
   Review of *Pickwick Papers*, 1838

Antiphanes of Macedonia
Idly inquisitive tribe of grammarians, who dig up the poetry of others by the roots…Get away, bugs, that bite secretly at the eloquent.
   Greek Anthology

Walter Bagehot
A schoolmaster should have an atmosphere of awe, and walk wonderingly, as if he was amazed at being himself.
   Literary Studies

Henry Peter Brougham, 1st Baron Brougham and Vaux
The schoolmaster is abroad, and I trust to him, armed with his primer, against the soldier in full military array.
   House of Commons speech, 1828

Robert Burns
Thou eunuch of language: thou butcher, imbruing thy hands in the bowels of orthography: thou arch-heretic in pronunciation: thou pitchpipe of affected emphasis: thou carpenter, mortising the awkward joints of jarring sentences: thou squeaking dissonance of cadence: thou

pimp of gender: thou scape-gallows from the land of syntax: thou
scavenger of mood and tense: thou murderous accoucheur of infant
learning: thou ignis fatuus, misleading the steps of benighted
ignorance: thou pickle-herring in the puppet-show of nonsense.
  [On an unidentified critic]

Critics!—appall'd I venture on the name,
Those cut-throat bandits in the paths of fame.
  Second Epistle to Robert Graham of Fintry

His locked, letter'd, braw brass collar,
Show'd him the gentleman and scholar.
  The Twa Dogs

Robert Burton
And to this day is every scholar poor;
Gross gold from them runs headlong to the door.
  Anatomy of Melancholy

George Gordon (Noel) Byron, 6th Lord Byron
With just enough of learning to misquote.
  English Bards and Scotch Reviewers

Thomas Carlyle
Respectable Professors of the Dismal Science.
  Latter-Day Pamphlets

George Chapman
And let a scholar all Earth's volumes carry,
He will be but a walking dictionary.
  Tears of Peace

Charles Churchill
Dull, superstitious readers they deceive,
Who pin their easy faith on critic's sleeve,
And knowing nothing, every thing believe.
  The Apology

Though by whim, envy, or resentment led,
They damn those authors whom they never read.
  The Candidate

Confucius
The scholar who cherishes the love of comfort, is not fit to be deemed a scholar.
Analects

Destouches [Philippe Néricault]
Criticism is easy, art is difficult.
Le Glorieux

Ralph Waldo Emerson
The man who can make hard things easy is the educator.
Journals, 1861

The scholar must be a solitary, modest, and charitable soul. He must embrace solitude as a bride…that he may become acquainted with his thoughts.
Nature, Addresses, and Lectures: Literary Ethics

I offer perpetual congratulation to the scholar; he has drawn the white lot in life.
Lectures and Biographical Sketches: The Man of Letters

George Savile, 1st Marquis of Halifax
The vanity of teaching often tempteth a man to forget he is a blockhead.
Works

Oliver Wendell Holmes
The world's great men have not commonly been great scholars, nor its great scholars great men.
The Autocrat of the Breakfast Table

Elbert Hubbard
Now owls are not really wise—they only look that way. The owl is a sort of college professor.
Epigrams

Aldous (Leonard) Huxley
The solemn foolery of scholarship for scholarship's sake.
The Perennial Philosophy

Dr Samuel Johnson

You may abuse a tragedy, though you cannot write one. You may scold a carpenter who has made you a bad table, though you cannot make a table. It is not your trade to make tables.

   Boswell's *Life of Johnson*

Mark what ills the scholar's life assail,
Toil, envy, want, the patron, and the jail.
   The Vanity of Human Wishes

Ben(jamin) Jonson

Very few men are wise by their own counsel; or learned by their own teaching. For he that was only taught by himself, had a fool to his master.
   Explorata: Consilia

H(enry) L(ouis) Mencken

The average schoolmaster is and always must be essentially an ass, for how can one imagine an intelligent man engaging in so puerile an avocation.
   Prejudices

Mohammed

The ink of the scholar is more sacred than the blood of the martyr.
   Tribute to Reason

Alexander Pope

Let such teach others who themselves excel,
And censure freely who have written well.
   Essay on Criticism

Some have at first for Wits then Poets past,
Turn'd Critics next, and prov'd plain fools at last.
   Ibid

The generous Critic fann'd the Poet's fire,
And taught the world with reason to admire.
   Ibid

Hugh Rhodes

Men learn when they teach.
   Boke of Nurture

George Bernard Shaw
A drama critic is a man who leaves no turn unstoned.
  New York Times, 1950

He who can, does. He who cannot, teaches.
  Maxims for Revolutionists

Sydney Smith
I never read a book before reviewing it; it prejudices a man so.
  The Smith of Smiths by H. Pearson

Oscar (Fingall O'Flahertie Wills) Wilde
Everybody who is incapable of learning has taken to teaching.
  The Decay of Lying

John Wolcot
Proud to find faults and raptured with defect! [Of critics.]
  Benevolent Epistle to Sylvanus Urban

Ignorance & Learning

Joseph Addison
Education is a companion which no misfortune can depress, no crime can destroy, no enemy can alienate, no despotism can enslave. At home a friend, abroad an introduction, in solitude a solace, and in society an ornament. It chastens vice, it guides virtue, it gives, at once, grace and government to genius. Without it, what is man? A splendid slave, a reasoning savage.
The Spectator

(Amos) Bronson Alcott
To be ignorant of one's ignorance is the malady of the ignorant.
Table Talk: Discourse

Francis Bacon
I have taken all knowledge to be my province.
Letter, 1592

Sir J(ames) M(atthew) Barrie
Facts were never pleasing to him. He acquired them with reluctance and got rid of them with relief. He was never on terms with them until he had stood them on their heads.
Love Me Never or For Ever

The Bible
He that hath knowledge spareth his words.
Proverbs 17

Paul, thou art beside thyself; much learning doth make thee mad.
Acts 26

Ambrose (Gwinett) Bierce
Education: that which discloses to the wise and disguises from the foolish their lack of understanding.
The Devil's Dictionary

Erudition: dust shaken out of a book into an empty skull.
Ibid

Learning: the kind of ignorance distinguishing the studious.
Ibid

Charlotte Brontë

Prejudices, it is well known, are most difficult to eradicate from the heart whose soil has never been loosened or fertilized by education; they grow there, firm as weeds among stones.
Jane Eyre

Henry Peter Brougham, 1st Baron Brougham and Vaux

Education makes a people easy to lead, but difficult to drive; easy to govern, but impossible to enslave.
Attributed

Charles V [Charles the Wise]

I speak Spanish to God, Italian to women, French to men, and German to my horse.
Attributed

Sir Winston (Leonard Spencer) Churchill

It is a good thing for an uneducated man to read books of quotations...The quotations when engraved upon the memory give you good thoughts. They also make you anxious to read the authors and look for more.
Roving Commission: My Early Life

Confucius

Learning without thought is labour lost; thought without learning is perilous.
Analects

Charles Dickens

A smattering of everything and a knowledge of nothing.
Sketches by Boz

"Now what I want is, Facts. Teach these boys and girls nothing but

Facts. Facts alone are wanted in life. Plant nothing else, and root out everything else...Stick to Facts, sir!"
  Hard Times

Diogenes
The foundation of every state is the education of its youth.
  Stobaeus' *Florilegium*

Diogenes Laertius
On one occasion Aristotle was asked how much educated men were superior to those uneducated; "As much," said he, "as the living are to the dead."
  Lives of Eminent Philosophers

Henry Fielding
Public schools are the nurseries of all vice and immorality.
  Joseph Andrews

Martin H. Fischer
All the world's a laboratory to the inquiring mind.
  Fischerisms by Howard Fabing and Ray Marr

Thomas Fuller
Learning hath gained most by those books by which the printers have lost.
  The Holy State and the Profane State: Of Books

James Abram Garfield
Next in importance to freedom and justice is popular education, without which neither freedom nor justice can be permanently maintained.
  Letter of Acceptance, 1880

Oliver Goldsmith
In arguing too, the parson own'd his skill,
For e'en though vanquish'd, he could argue still;
While words of learned length and thund'ring sound
Amazed the gazing rustics rang'd around,
And still they gaz'd, and still the wonder grew,

That one small head could carry all he knew.
   The Deserted Village

William Hazlitt
It is better to be able neither to read nor write than to be able to do nothing else.
   Table Talk: On the Ignorance of the Learned

Georg Wilhelm Friedrich Hegel
But what experience and history teach is this, that peoples and government have never learned anything from history.
   The Philosophy of History

William Harvey
All we know is still infinitely less than all that still remains unknown.
   De Motu Cordis et Sanguinis

Thomas Hughes
Life isn't all beer and skittles; but beer and skittles, or something better of the same sort, must form a good part of every Englishman's education.
   Tom Brown's Schooldays

Thomas Henry Huxley
The great tragedy of Science: the slaying of a beautiful hypothesis by an ugly fact.
   'Biogenesis and Abigenesis'

Dr Samuel Johnson
Integrity without knowledge is weak and useless, and knowledge without integrity is dangerous and dreadful.
   Rasselas

A man is in general better pleased when he has a good dinner upon his table than when his wife talks Greek.
   Johnsonian Miscellanies

Maimonides [Moses ben Maimon]
Teach thy tongue to say "I do not know".

Christopher Marlowe
I count religion but a childish toy,
And hold there is no sin but ignorance.
  The Jew of Malta

William Lamb, 2nd Viscount Melbourne
I don't know, Ma'am, why they make all this fuss about education; none of the Pagets can read or write, and they get on well enough.
  Remark to Queen Victoria

Alexander Pope
A little learning is a dangerous thing;
Drink deep, or taste not the Pierian spring:
  Essay on Criticism

The proper study of mankind is man.
  Moral Essays

Sir Walter Alexander Raleigh
In an examination those who do not wish to know ask questions of those who cannot tell.
  Laughter from a Cloud: Some Thoughts on Examinations

Bertrand Russell
Science is what you know, philosophy is what you don't know.

Sir Walter Scott
All men who have turned out worth anything have had the chief hand in their own education.
  Letter, 1830

William Shakespeare
Away with him, away with him! he speaks Latin.
  King Henry VI, Part II 4

John Sheffield, 1st Duke of Buckingham and Normanby
Learn to write well, or not to write at all.
  Essay on Satire

Socrates
There is only one good, knowledge, and one evil, ignorance.
Lives of Eminent Philosophers by Diogenes Laertius

Herbert Spencer
Science is organized knowledge.
Essays on Education

Charles Maurice de Talleyrand-Perigord
Ils n'ont rien appris, ni rien oublié.
They have learned nothing and forgotten nothing.
Attributed

Alfred, Lord Tennyson
To follow knowledge like a sinking star,
Beyond the utmost bound of human thought.
Ulysses

George Macaulay Trevelyan
Education…has produced a vast population able to read but unable to distinguish what is worth reading.
English Social History

Oscar (Fingall O'Flahertie Wills) Wilde
Education is an admirable thing, but it is well to remember from time to time that nothing that is worth knowing can be taught.
Intentions: The Critic as Artist

Edward Young
Some for renown, on scraps of learning dote,
And think they grow immortal as they quote.
Love of Fame

Politics & Politicians

John Emerich Edward Dalberg, 1st Baron Acton
Power tends to corrupt, and absolute power corrupts absolutely.
  Letter to Bishop Creighton, 1887

Aristophanes
You have all the characteristics of a popular politician: a horrible
voice, bad breeding, and a vulgar manner.
  Knights

Francis Bacon
It is as hard and severe a thing to be a true politician as to be truly moral.
  The Advancement of Learning

Aneurin Bevan
We know what happens to people who stay in the middle of the road.
They get run over.
  The Observer, 1953

Ambrose (Gwinett) Bierce
Elector: one who enjoys the sacred privilege of voting for the man of
another man's choice.
  The Devil's Dictionary

Politics: a strife of interests masquerading as a contest of principles.
The conduct of public affairs for private advantage.
  Ibid

Otto von Bismarck
Politics is the doctrine of the possible, the attainable.
  Speech, 1863

Winston (Leonard Spencer) Churchill
Politics are almost as exciting as war, and quite as dangerous. In war

you can only be killed once, but in politics many times.
  Said 1920

Ralph Waldo Emerson
Politics is a deleterious profession, like some poisonous handicrafts.
  The Conduct of Life

John Kenneth Galbraith
Politics is not the art of the possible. It consists in choosing between
the disastrous and the unpalatable.
  Ambassador's Journal

John Gay
That politician tops his part,
Who readily can lie with art.
  Fables

Sir William Schwenck Gilbert
I always voted at my party's call,
And I never thought of thinking for myself at all.
  HMS Pinafore

Isaac Goldberg
Diplomacy is to do and say
The nastiest thing in the nicest way.
  The Reflex

Thomas Hardy
When shall the softer, saner politics,
Whereof we dream, have play in each proud land?
  Departure

Richard Hooker
He that goeth about to persuade a multitude, that they are not so
well governed as they ought to be, shall never want attentive and
favourable hearers.
  Laws of Ecclesiastical Polity

Thomas Jefferson
I have no ambition to govern men. It is a painful and thankless office.
   Letter, 1796

Politics is such a torment that I would advise every one I love not to mix with it.
   Ibid, 1800

Dr Samuel Johnson
Why, Sir, most schemes of political improvement are very laughable things.
   Boswell's *Life of Johnson*

John Maynard Keynes, 1st Baron Keynes of Tilton
This long run is a misleading guide to current affairs. In the long run we are all dead.
   A Tract on Monetary Reform

Thomas Babington Macaulay, 1st Baron Macaulay
Timid and interested politicians think much more about the security of their seats than about the security of their country.
   House of Commons speech, 1842

Thomas Moore
The minds of some of our own statesmen, like the pupil of the human eye, contract themselves the more, the strong light there is shed upon them.
   Corruption and Intolerance, Preface

Wendell Phillips
Politicians are like the bones of a horse's foreshoulder—not a straight one in it.
   Speech, 1864

Sir John Robert Seeley
History is past politics and politics present history.
   The Growth of British Policy

William Shakespeare
Get thee glass eyes;
And, like a scurvy politician, seem
To see the things thou dost not.
King Lear 4

Robert Louis Stevenson
Politics is perhaps the only profession for which no preparation is thought necessary.
Familiar Studies of Men and Books: Yoshida-Torajiro

Jonathan Swift
Politics, as the word is understood, are nothing but corruptions.
Thoughts on Various Subjects

Margaret (Hilda) Thatcher
Anyway, I wouldn't want to be Prime Minister, you have to give yourself 100 per cent.
The Sunday Telegraph, 1969

James Grover Thurber
If you can't stand the heat, get out of the kitchen.
Mr Citizen

Voltaire [François Marie Arouet]
The pleasure of governing must certainly be exquisite if we may judge from the vast numbers who are eager to be concerned with it.
Philisophical Dictionary

John Webster
A politician imitates the Devil, as the Devil imitates a cannon: wheresoever he comes to do mischief, he comes with his backside towards you.
The White Devil

Government & State

Fisher Ames
A monarchy is a merchantman which sails well, but will sometimes strike on a rock, and go to the bottom; a republic is a raft which will never sink, but then your feet are always in the water.
   House of Representatives speech, 1795

Susan B(rownell) Anthony
The true Republic: men, their rights and nothing more; women, their rights and nothing less.
   Said 1872

Aristotle
A democracy is a government in the hands of men of low birth, no property, and vulgar employments.
   Politics

Clement Richard Attlee, 1st Earl Attlee
Democracy means government by discussion, but it is only effective if you can stop people talking.
   Anatomy of Britain

Sir William Blackstone
That the king can do no wrong, is a necessary and fundamental principle of the English constitution.
   Commentaries

(John) Anthony Burgess (Wilson)
The U.S. Presidency is a Tudor monarchy plus telephones.
   Writers at Work

Sir Charles Pratt, 1st Earl Camden
The British parliament has no right to tax the Americans...Taxation

and representation are inseparably united. God hath joined them: no
British parliament can put them asunder.
  House of Lords speech, 1765

G(ilbert) K(eith) Chesterton
Democracy means government by the uneducated, while aristocracy
means government by the badly educated.
  New York Times, 1931

You can never have a revolution in order to establish a democracy.
You must have a democracy in order to have a revolution.
  Tremendous Trifles

Winston (Leonard Spencer) Churchill
It has been said that democracy is the worst form of government,
except for all those other forms that have been tried from time to
time.
  House of Commons speech, 1947

Confucius
In a country well governed, poverty is something to be ashamed of.
In a country badly governed, wealth is something to be ashamed of.
  Analects

James Fenimore Cooper
Contact with the affairs of state is one of the most corrupting of the
influences to which men are exposed.
  The American Democrat

Benjamin Disraeli, 1st Earl of Beaconsfield
No Government can be long secure without a formidable Opposition.
  Coningsby

Conservatism discards Prescription, shrinks from Principle,
disavows Progress; having rejected all respect for antiquity, it offers
no redress for the present, and makes no preparation for the future.
  Ibid

A Conservative government is an organized hypocrisy.
  House of Commons speech, 1845

Albert Einstein
The State is made for man, not man for the State.
The World As I See It

Benjamin Franklin
In rivers and bad governments the lightest things swim at the top.
Poor Richard's Almanack 1754

Milton Friedman
Governments never learn. Only people learn.
The Observer, 1980

The government solution to a problem is usually as bad as the problem.
Attributed

David Hume
Nothing appears more surprising to those who consider human affairs with a philosophical eye, than the easiness with which the many are governed by the few.
Essays Moral and Political

Thomas Jefferson
The care of human life and happiness, and not their destruction, is the first and only legitimate object of good government.
Speech in Maryland, 1809

Abraham Lincoln
No man is good enough to govern another man without that other's consent.
Speech, 1854

The ballot is stronger than the bullet.
Ibid, 1856

As I would not be a slave, so I would not be a master. This expresses my idea of democracy.
Said when Vice-President, 1858

Louis XIV
L'Etat, c'est moi.

I am the State.
  Attributed

Niccolo Machiavelli
All well-governed states and wise princes have taken care not to reduce the nobility to despair, nor the people to discontent.
  The Prince

Joseph Marie, Comte de Maistre
Toute nation a le gouvernement qu'elle merite.
Every nation has the government it deserves.
  Letter from Russia, 1811

Karl Marx and Friedrich Engels
In this sense, the theory of the Communists may be summed up in the single sentence: Abolition of private property.
  The Communist Manifesto

John Stuart Mill
The worth of a state, in the long run, is the worth of the individuals composing it.
  On Liberty

Charles Louis de Secondat, Baron de Montesquieu
When a government lasts a long while, it deteriorates by insensible degrees.
  The Spirit of the Laws

The deterioration of every government begins with the decay of the principles on which it was founded.
  Ibid

Jawaharlal Nehru
The forces of a capitalist society, if left unchecked, tend to make the rich richer and the poor poorer.
  Credo

James Otis
Taxation without representation is tyranny.
  Attributed, 1763

Thomas Paine
Society in every state is a blessing, but government, even in its best state, is but a necessary evil; in its worst state, an intolerable one.
Common Sense

William Penn
No system of government was ever so ill devised that, under proper men, it wouldn't work well enough.
Some Fruits of Solitude

Let the people think they govern and they will be governed.
Ibid

Plato
Democracy…is a charming form of government, full of variety and disorder, and dispensing a kind of quality to equals and unequals alike.
The Republic

The rulers of the State are the only ones who should have the privilege of lying, either at home or abroad; they may be allowed to lie for the good of the State.
Ibid

Our object in the construction of the state is the greatest happiness of the whole, and not that of any one class.
Ibid

Alexander Pope
The right divine of kings to govern wrong.
The Dunciad

Jean Jacques Rousseau
If there were a nation of gods they would be governed democratically, but so perfect a government is not suitable to men.
The Social Contract

William Shakespeare
Not all the water in the rude rough sea
Can wash the balm from an anointed king.
King Richard II 3

Uneasy lies the head that wears a crown.
  King Henry IV, Part II 3

Something is rotten in the state of Denmark.
  Hamlet 1

George Bernard Shaw
Democracy substitutes election by the incompetent many for appointment by the corrupt few.
  Man and Superman: Maxims for Revolutionists

Herbert Spencer
The Republican form of government is the highest form of government; but because of this it requires the highest type of human nature—a type nowhere at present existing.
  Essays: The Americans

Voltaire [François Marie Arouet]
Democracy seems suitable only to a very little country.
  Philosohical Dictionary

In general, the art of government consists in taking as much money as possible from one class of citizens to give to the other.
  Ibid

Freedom & Oppression

Joseph Addison
A day, an hour of virtuous liberty
Is worth a whole eternity in bondage.
  Cato

St Augustine of Hippo
He that is good is free, though he be a slave; that is evil is a slave,
though he be a king.
  The City of God

Bertrand Barère de Vieuzac
L'arbre de la liberté ne croît qu'arrosé par le sang des tyrans.
The tree of liberty grows only when watered by the blood of tyrants.
  Speech, 1792

The Bible
The truth shall make you free.
  John 8

With a great sum obtained I this freedom. And Paul said, But I was
free born.
  Acts 22

Edmund Burke
Abstract liberty, like other mere abstractions, is not to be found.
  On Conciliation with America: The Thirteen Resolutions

Robert Burns
Freedom and whisky gang thegither,
Tak aff your dram!
  The Author's Earnest Cry and Prayer

Liberty's in every blow!—

Let us do or die!
Bruce before Bannockburn

A fig for those by law protected!
Liberty's a glorious feast!
Love and Liberty or The Jolly Beggars

We labour soon, we labour late,
To feed the titled knave, man,
And a' the comfort we're to get,
Is that ayont the grave, man.
The Tree of Liberty

George Gordon (Noel), 6th Lord Byron
Yet, Freedom! yet thy banner, torn, but flying,
Streams like the thunderstorm against the wind.
Childe Harold's Pilgrimage

Hereditary Bondsmen! know ye not
Who would be free themselves must strike the blow?
Ibid

Albert Camus
Fascism...represents the exaltation of the executioner by the
executioner....Russian Communism...represents the exaltation of the
executioner by the victim. The former never dreamed of liberating
all men, but only of liberating the few by subjugating the rest. The
latter, in its most profound principle, aims at liberating all men by
provisionally enslaving them all.
The Rebel

Lydia Maria Child
They [slaves] have stabbed themselves for freedom—jumped into
the waves for freedom—fought like very tigers for freedom! But
they have been hung, and burned, and shot—and their tyrants have
been their historians.
An Appeal on Behalf of That Class of Americans called Africans

William Cowper
Freedom has a thousand charms to show,

That slaves, howe'er contented, never know.
  Table-Talk

Slaves cannot breathe in England; if their lungs
Receive our air, that moment they are free;
They touch our country, and their shackles fall.
  The Task: The Timepiece

John Philpot Curran

The condition upon which God hath given liberty to men is eternal
vigilance; which condition if he break, servitude is at once the
consequence of his crime, and the punishment of his guilt.
  Speech, 1790

Charles Dickens

Oh, let us love our occupations,
Bless the squire and his relations,
Live upon our daily rations,
And always know our proper stations.
  The Chimes

John Dryden

I am as free as Nature first made man,
Ere the base laws of servitude began,
When wild in woods the noble savage ran.
  The Conquest of Granada

Paul Laurence Dunbar

It is not a carol of joy or glee,
But a prayer that he sends from his heart's deep core…
I know why the caged bird sings!
  Sympathy

Benjamin Franklin

They that can give up essential liberty to obtain a little temporary
safety deserve neither liberty nor safely.
  Historical Review of Pennsylvania

Oliver Goldsmith
This is Liberty-hall, gentlemen.
  She Stoops to Conquer

Samuel Gompers
Show me the country that has no strikes and I'll show the country in
which there is no liberty.
  Speech

W(illiam) E(rnest) Henley
I am the master of my fate:
I am the captain of my soul.
  Echoes: In Memoriam

Patrick Henry
Is life so dear, or peace so sweet, as to be purchased at the price of
chains and slavery?...as for me, give me liberty or give me death!
  Speech, 1775

Oliver Wendell Holmes
The freeman casting with unpurchased hand
The vote that shakes the turrets of the land.
  Poetry: a Metrical Essay

Henrik Ibsen
The most dangerous enemy to truth and freedom in our midst is the
compact majority. Yes, the damned, compact, liberal majority.
  An Enemy of the People

You should never put on your best trousers when you go out to fight
for freedom and truth.
  Ibid

James I
The bird, the beast, the fish eke in the sea,
They live in freedom everich in his kind;
And I a man, and lackith liberty.
  The Kingis Quair

Thomas Jefferson
The God who gave us life gave us liberty at the same time.
Summary View of the Rights of British America

We hold these truths to be self-evident,—that all men are created equal; that they are endowed by their Creator with certain inalienable rights; that among these are life, liberty, and the pursuit of happiness.
The Declaration of Independence

The tree of liberty must be refreshed from time to time with the blood of patriots and tyrants. It is its natural manure.
Letter, 1787

Martin Luther King
I have a dream that one day on the red hills of Georgia the sons of former slaves and the sons of former slave-owners will be able to sit down together at the table of brotherhood.
Speech, 1963

Emma Lazarus
Give me your tired, your poor,
Your huddled masses yearning to breathe free,
The wretched refuse of your teeming shore.
The New Colossus (inscribed on the pedestal of the Statue of Liberty)

Nikolai Lenin [Vladimir Ilyich Ulyanov]
It is true that liberty is precious—so precious that it must be rationed.
Attributed

Abraham Lincoln
That this nation, under God, shall have a new birth of freedom, and that government of the people, by the people, and for the people, shall not perish from the earth.
The Gettysburg Address, 1863

Whenever I hear anyone arguing for slavery, I feel a strong impulse to see it tried on him personally.
Address to an Indiana regiment, 1865

Karl Marx and **Friedrich Engels**
The workers have nothing to lose but their chains. They have a world to gain. Workers of the world, unite!
The Communist Manifesto

John Stuart Mill
The liberty of the individual must be thus far limited; he must not make himself a nuisance to other people.
On Liberty

John Milton
Give me the liberty to know, to utter, and to argue freely according to conscience, above all liberties.
Areopagitica

No man who knows aught, can be so stupid to deny that all men naturally were born free.
Tenure of Kings and Magistrates

Molière [Jean-Baptiste Poquelin]
Il se faut réserver une arrière boutique...en laquelle nous établissions notre vraie liberté.
We must keep a little back shop...where we may establish our own true liberty.
Essais

George Orwell [Eric Arthur Blair]
All animals are equal, but some animals are more equal than others.
Animal Farm

William Pitt the Younger
Necessity is the plea for every infringement of human freedom. It is the argument of tyrants; it is the creed of slaves.
House of Commons speech, 1783

Marie Jeanne Philipon Roland de la Platière
O Liberté! que de crimes on commet en ton nom!
O Liberty! what crimes are committed in your name!
From the scaffold, seeing a statue of Liberty

Jean Jacques Rousseau
L'homme est né libre, et partout il est dans les fers.
Man is born free, and everywhere he is in chains.
   The Social Contract

George Bernard Shaw
Liberty means responsibility. That is why most men dread it.
   Man and Superman: Maxims for Revolutionists

Herbert Spencer
No one can be perfectly free till all are free.
   Social Statics

James Thomson and **David Malloch** or **Mallet**
"Rule, Britannia, rule the waves;
Britons never will be slaves."
   Alfred: A Masque

Voltaire [François Marie Arouet]
La Liberté est née en Angleterre des querelles des tyrans.
Liberty was born in England from the quarrels of tyrants.
   Lettres Philosophiques

George Washington
Liberty, when it begins to take root, is a plant of rapid growth.
   Letter, 1788

Thomas Woodrow Wilson
The history of liberty is a history of resistance.
   Speech, 1812

William Wordsworth
We must be free or die, who speak the tongue
That Shakespeare spake; the faith and morals hold
Which Milton held.
   Sonnet: It is not to be thought of

Lawyers & the Law

Francis Bacon
One of the Seven was wont to say: "That laws were like cobwebs; where the small flies were caught, and the great brake through."
Apothegms

Henry Ward Beecher
Riches without law are more dangerous than is poverty without law.
Proverbs from Plymouth Pulpit

Jeremy Bentham
Every law is an evil, for every law is an infraction of liberty.
Principles of Morals and Legislation

The Bible
For as many as have sinned without law shall also perish without law: and as many as have sinned in the law shall be judged by the law.
Romans 2

These, not having the law, are a law unto themselves.
Ibid 2

Ambrose (Gwinett) Bierce
Lawyer: one skilled in circumvention of the law.
The Devil's Dictionary

Litigation: a machine which you go into as a pig and come out of as a sausage.
Ibid

Henry Peter Brougham, Baron Brougham and Vaux
All we see about us, Kings, Lords, and Commons, the whole machinery of the State, all the apparatus of the system, and its varied workings, end in simply bringing twelve good men into a box.
The Present State of the Law

William Camden
Agree, for the law is costly.
Remains Concerning Britain

Charles Dickens
"If the law supposes that," said Mr Bumble..."the law is a ass—a idiot."
Oliver Twist

George Eliot [Mary Ann Evans]
The law's made to take care o' raskills.
The Mill on the Floss

Anatole France [Jacques Anatole Thibault]
The law, in its majestic equality, forbids the rich as well as the poor to sleep under bridges, to beg in the streets, and to steal bread.
Cournos' *Modern Plutarch*

Christopher (Harris) Fry
I know I am not
A practical person; legal matters and so forth
Are Greek to me, except, of course,
That I understand Greek.
The Lady's not for Burning

Sir William Schwenck Gilbert
And many a burglar I've restored
  To his friends and his relations.
Trial by Jury

When constabulary duty's to be done,
A policeman's lot is not a happy one.
The Pirates of Penzance

Oliver Goldsmith
Laws grind the poor, and rich men rule the law.
The Traveller

Ulysses S(impson) Grant
I know of no method to secure the repeal of bad or obnoxious laws

so effective as their stringent execution.
Inaugural address, 1869

Charles Macklin
The law is a sort of hocus-pocus science, that smiles in yer face while it picks yer pocket: and the glorious uncertainty of it is of mair use to the professors than the justice of it.
Love à la Mode

Charles Louis de Secondat, Baron de Montesquieu
Useless laws weaken the necessary laws.
The Spirit of the Laws

Christopher North [John Wilson]
Laws were made to be broken.
Noctes Ambrosianae

William Pitt the Elder
Where law ends, tyranny begins.
House of Lords speech, 1770

Jean Jacques Rousseau
Good laws lead to the making of better ones; bad ones bring about worse.
The Social Contract

John Selden
Ignorance of the law excuses no man; not that all men know the law, but because 'tis an excuse every man will plead, and no man can tell how to refute him.
Table Talk: Judgments

William Shakespeare
The first thing to do is kill all the lawyers.
King Henry VI, Part II 4

Old father antic the law
King Henry IV, Part I 1

Justice & Mercy

Martin Luther King
Injustice anywhere is a threat to justice everywhere.
  Letter, 1963

Francis Bacon
Revenge is a kind of wild justice.
  Essays: Of Revenge

Guillaume de Salluste, Seigneur du Bartas
Mercy and Justice, marching cheek by jowl.
  Divine Weeks and Works: Week 1, Day 1

Ambrose (Gwinett) Bierce
Justice: a commodity which in a more or less adulterated condition
the State sells to the citizen as a reward for his allegiance, taxes and
personal service.
  The Devil's Dictionary

Mercy: an attribute beloved of detected offenders.
  Ibid

Albert Camus
Absolute freedom mocks at justice. Absolute justice denies freedom.
  The Rebel

Marcus Tullius Cicero
The fundamentals of justice are that no one shall suffer wrong, and
that the public good be served.
  De Officiis

John Dryden
Our mercy is become our crime.
  Absalom and Achitophel

George Eliot [Mary Ann Evans]
There is a mercy which is weakness, and even treason against the
common good.
Romola

Henry Fielding
Thwackum was for doing justice, and leaving mercy to heaven.
Tom Jones

Lord Gordon Hewart
It is not merely of some importance but is of fundamental
importance that justice should not only be done, but should
manifestly and undoubtedly be seen to be done.
Jackson's *The Chief*

Richard Hovey
Ah, to be just, as well as kind,—
It costs so little and so much!
Contemporaries

Walter Savage Landor
Delay of justice is injustice.
Imaginary Conversations: Peter Leopold and President Du Paty

James Russell Lowell
Exact justice is commonly more merciful in the long run than pity,
for it tends to foster in men those stronger qualities which make
them good citizens.
Among My Books: Dante

Magna Carta
To no one will we sell, to no one will we refuse or delay right or
justice.
Article 40

Lord Mansfield
Consider what you think justice requires, and decide accordingly.
But never give your reasons; for your judgement will probably be

right, but your reasons will certainly be wrong.
  Campbell's *Lives of the Chief Justices*

H(enry) L(ouis) Mencken
Injustice is relatively easy to bear; what stings is justice.
  Prejudices

John Milton
Yet I shall temper so
Justice with mercy, as may illustrate most
Them fully satisfied, and thee appease.
  Paradise Lost

Blaise Pascal
Justice without strength is helpless, strength without justice is
tyrannical...Unable to make what is just strong, we have made what
is strong just.
  Pensées

William Shakespeare
The quality of mercy is not strain'd,
It droppeth as the gentle rain from heaven.
  The Merchant of Venice 3

But mercy is above this sceptred sway;
It is enthroned in the hearts of kings,
It is an attribute to God himself;
And earthly power doth then show likest God's
When mercy seasons justice.
  Ibid 4

Sparing justice feeds iniquity.
  The Rape of Lucrece

William Watson
Fiat justitia et ruant coeli.
Let justice be done though the heavens fall.
  Questions Concerning Religion and State

Oscar (Fingall O'Flahertie Wills) Wilde
For Man's grim Justice goes its way,
  And will not swerve aside:
It slays the weak, it slays the strong,
  It has a deadly stride.
  The Ballad of Reading Goal

Mary Wollstonecraft
It is justice, not charity, that is wanting in the world.
  A Vindication of the Rights of Women

Crime & Punishment

Woody Allen [Allen Stewart Konigsberg]
I think crime pays. The hours are good, you travel a lot.
  Take the Money and Run

Francis Bacon
Opportunity makes a thief.
  Letter, 1598

Jeremy Bentham
All punishment is mischief; all punishment in itself is evil.
  Principles of Morals and Legislation

The Bible
My father hath chastised you with whips, but I will chastise you with
scorpions.
  I Kings 12

Stolen waters are sweet.
  Proverbs 9

Charles Synge Christopher Bowen, Baron Bowen of Colwood
The rain it raineth on the just
  And also on the unjust fella:
But chiefly on the just, because
  The unjust steals the just's umbrella.
  Sichel's *Sands of Time*

Marcus Tullius Cicero
The greatest incitement to crime is the hope of escaping punishment.
  Pro Milone

Let the punishment be equal with the offence.
  De Legibus

William Congreve
See how love and murder will out.
The Double Dealer

Thomas De Quincey
If once a man indulge himself in murder, very soon he comes to
think little of robbing; and from robbing he next comes to drinking
and Sabbath-breaking, and from that to incivility and procrastination.
Murder Considered as One of the Fine Arts

Sir Arthur Conan Doyle
Singularity is almost invariably a clue. The more featureless and
commonplace a crime is, the more difficult it is to bring it home.
The Adventures of Sherlock Holmes

George Eliot [Mary Ann Evans]
That is the bitterest of all,—to wear the yoke of our wrong-doing.
Daniel Deronda

Ralph Waldo Emerson
Wherever a man commits a crime, God finds a witness…Every
secret crime has its reporter.
Uncollected Lectures: Natural Religion

There is no den in the wide world to hide a rogue. Commit a crime
and the earth is made of glass.
Essays, First Series: Compensation

Joseph Fouché
C'est plus qu'un crime; c'est une faute.
It is worse than a crime; it is a blunder.
Memoirs

Sir William Schwenck Gilbert
   My object all sublime
   I shall achieve in time—
To let the punishment fit the crime.
The Mikado 2

George Herbert
Punishment is lame, but it comes.
Jacula Prudentum

E(dgar) W(atson) Howe
The greatest punishment is to be despised by your neighbors, the world, and members of your family.
Howe's Monthly

Dr Samuel Johnson
Depend upon it, sir, when a man knows he is to be hanged in a fortnight, it concentrates his mind wonderfully.
Boswell's *Life of Johnson*

Juvenal [Decimus Junius Juvenalis]
Quisnam hominum est quem tu contentum videris uno Flagitio?
What man have you ever seen who was contented with one crime only?
Satires

Abraham Lincoln
He reminds me of the man who murdered both his parents, and then, when sentence was about to be pronounced, pleaded for mercy on the grounds that he was an orphan.
Gross's *Lincoln's Own Stories*

Napoleon I [Napoleon Bonaparte]
The contagion of crime is like that of the plague.
Sayings of Napoleon

Alexander Pope
The hungry judges soon the sentence sign,
And wretches hang that jurymen may dine.
The Rape of the Lock

Robert Rice
Crime is a logical extension of the sort of behaviour that is often considered perfectly respectable in legitimate business.
The Business of Crime

Seneca

There is no crime without a precedent.
Hippolytus

Cui podest scelus Is fecit.
Who profits by a crime commits the crime.
Medea

William Shakespeare

The most peaceable way for you, if you do take a thief, is to let him show himself what he is and steal out of your company.
Much Ado About Nothing 3

Murder most foul, as in the best it is.
Hamlet 1

It hath the primal eldest curse upon't,
A brother's murder.
Ibid 3

Every true man's apparel fits your thief.
Measure for Measure 4

Thou shalt be whipp'd with wire, and stew'd in brine,
Smarting in lingering pickle.
Antony and Cleopatra 2

Bid that welcome
Which comes to punish us, and we punish it
Seeming to bear it lightly.
Ibid 2

Herbert Spencer

Every unpunished delinquency has a family of delinquencies.
The Study of Sociology, Postscript

Publilius Syrus

Injuriam ipse facias ubi non vindices.
You yourself are guilty of a crime when you do not punish crime.
Sententiæ

Qui culpæ ignoscit uni, suadet pluribus.
Pardon one offense and you encourage the commission of many.
  Ibid

Voltaire [François Marie Arouet]
Fear follows crime, and is its punishment.
  Semiramis

It is better to risk saving a guilty person than to condemn an innocent one.
  Zadig

Mary Wollstonecraft
Executions, far from being useful examples to the survivors, have, I am persuaded, a quite contrary effect, by hardening the heart thay ought to terrify.
  Letters written in Sweden, Norway and Denmark

God, Faith & Religion

Lancelot Andrewes
The nearer the Church the further from God.
  Sermon

St Augustine of Hippo
We can know what God is not, but we cannot know what he is.
  De Trinitate

There is no salvation outside the church.
  De Bapt.

Walter Bagehot
So long as there are earnest believers in the world, they will always
wish to punish opinions, even if their judgment tells them it is
unwise, and their conscience that it is wrong.
  Literary Studies

Honoré de Balzac
I believe in the incomprehensibility of God.
  Letter, 1837

The Bible
I know that my redeemer liveth, and that he shall stand at the latter
day upon the earth.
  Job 9

The Lord is my shepherd; I shall not want. He maketh me to lie
down in green pastures: he leadeth me beside the still waters. He
restoreth my soul: he leadeth me in the paths of righteousness for his
name's sake. Yea, though I walk through the valley of the shadow of
death, I will fear no evil: for thou art with me; thy rod and thy staff
they comfort me.
  Psalms 23

God is our refuge and strength, a very present help in trouble.
Ibid 46

I will lift up mine eyes unto the hills, from whence cometh my help.
My help cometh from the Lord, which made heaven and earth.
Ibid 121

The Lord shall preserve thy going out and thy coming in from this
time forth, and even for evermore.
Ibid

Fear God, and keep his commandments: for this is the whole duty of
man.
Ecclesiastes 12

Blessed are the poor in spirit: for theirs is the kingdom of heaven.
Blessed are they that mourn: for they shall be comforted. Blessed are
the meek: for they shall inherit the earth. Blessed are they which do
hunger and thirst after righteousness: for they shall be filled. Blessed
are the merciful: for they shall obtain mercy. Blessed are the pure in
heart: for they shall see God. Blessed are the peacemakers: for they
shall be called the children of God.
Matthew 5

Our Father which art in heaven, Hallowed be thy name. Thy
kingdom come. Thy will be done in earth, as it is in heaven. Give us
this day our daily bread. And forgive us our debts, as we forgive our
debtors. And lead us not into temptation, but deliver us from evil.
For thine is the kingdom, and the power, and the glory, for ever.
Amen.
Ibid 6

Thou art Peter, and upon this rock I will build my church; and the
gates of hell shall not prevail against it. And I will give unto thee the
keys of the kingdom of heaven.
Ibid 16

Verily I say unto you, Except ye be converted, and become as little
children, ye shall not enter into the kingdom of heaven.
Ibid 18

For many are called, but few are chosen.
  Ibid 22

The sabbath was made for man, and not man for the sabbath.
  Mark 2

Glory to God in the highest, and on earth peace, good will toward men.
  Luke 2

Likewise joy shall be in heaven over one sinner that repenteth, more than over ninety and nine just persons, which need no repentance.
  Ibid 15

In the beginning was the Word, and the Word was with God, and the Word was God.
  John 1

If God be for us, who can be against us?
  Romans 8

I have fought a good fight, I have finished my course, I have kept the faith.
  2 Timothy 4

Now faith is the substance of things hoped for, the evidence of things not seen.
  Hebrews 11

I am Alpha and Omega, the beginning and the ending, saith the Lord.
  Revelation 1

William Blake
I will not cease from mental fight,
  Nor shall my sword sleep in my hand,
Till we have built Jerusalem
  In England's green and pleasant land.
  Milton, Preface

Emily Jane Brontë
He was…the wearisomest, self-righteous pharisee that ever ransacked a Bible to rake the promises to himself and fling the curses on his neighbours.
  Wuthering Heights

Sir Thomas Browne
Persecution is a bad and indirect way to plant religion.
  Religio Medici

Robert Browning
I show you doubt, to prove that faith exists.
  Bishop Blougram's Apology

The lark's on the wing;
The snail's on the thorn:
God's in his heaven—
All's right with the world!
  Pippa Passes

Ah, but a man's reach should exceed his grasp,
Or what's a heaven for?
  Andrea del Sarto

Edmund Burke
Politics and the pulpit are terms that have little agreement.
  Reflections on the Revolution in France

Robert Burton
One religion is as true as another.
  The Anatomy of Melancholy

Roger, Comte de Bussy-Rabutin
As you know, God is usually on the side of the big squadrons and
against the small ones.
  Letter, 1677

Samuel Butler
An apology for the Devil: it must be remembered that we have heard
only one side of the case. God has written all the books.
  Note Books

An honest God's the noblest work of man.
  Further Extracts from the Note-Books

George Gordon (Noel), 6th Lord Byron
"Whom the gods love die young" was said of yore.
  Don Juan

Thomas Carlyle
The three great elements of modern civilization, Gunpowder,
Printing, and the Protestant Religion.
  Critical and Miscellaneous Essays: State of German Literature

Philip Dormer Stanhope, 4th Earl of Chesterfield
Religion is by no means a proper subject of conversation in a mixed
company.
  Letter to his godson

Marcus Tullius Cicero
Nature herself has imprinted on the minds of all the idea of a God.
  De Natura Deorum

Charles Caleb Colton
Men will wrangle for religion; write for it; fight for it; die for it;
anything but—live for it.
  Lacon

Sir Noel (Pierce) Coward
Life without faith is an arid business.
  Blithe Spirit

Daniel Defoe
And of all plagues with which mankind are curst,
Ecclesiastic tyranny's the worst.
  The True-Born Englishman

Charles Dickens
"God bless us every one!" said Tiny Tim.
  A Christmas Carol

Diogenes
I do not know whether there are gods, but there ought to be.
  Tertullian's *Ad Nationes*

John Dryden
Gods they had tried of every shape and size
That godsmiths could produce or priests devise.
  Absalom and Achitophel

Albert Einstein
Science without religion is lame, religion without science is blind.
Out of My Later Years

Henry Havelock Ellis
The whole religious complexion of the modern world is due to the absence from Jerusalem of a lunatic asylum.
Impressions and Comments

Ralph Waldo Emerson
Shove Jesus and Judas equally aside.
Essays, First Series: Self-Reliance

I like the silent church before the sevice begins, better than any preaching.
Ibid

Demonology is the shadow of theology.
Demonology

Empedocles
The nature of God is a circle of which the centre is everywhere and the circumference is nowhere.
Attributed

Epicurus
It is folly for a man to pray to the gods for that which he has the power to obtain for himself.
Vatican Sayings

Heinrich Heine
Christianity is an idea, and as such is indestructible and immortal, like every idea.
History of Religion and Philosophy in Germany

Henry II
Will no one free me of this turbulent priest [Thomas à Becket]?
Attributed

Thomas Hood
But now 'tis little joy

To know I'm farther off from heav'n
Than when I was a boy.
  I remember, I remember

Gerard Manley Hopkins
The world is charged with the grandeur of God.
  Poems: God's Grandeur

William Ralph Inge
The modern town-dweller has no God and no Devil; he lives without
awe, without admiration, without fear.
  Outspoken Essays: Our Present Discontents

Douglas William Jerrold
Religion's in the heart, not in the knees.
  The Devil's Ducat

Martin Luther
I cannot and I will not recant anything, for to go against conscience
is neither right nor safe. Here I stand. I cannot do otherwise. God
help me. Amen.
  Diet of Worms speech, 1521

Thomas Babington Macaulay, 1st Baron Macaulay
She [the Roman Catholic church] may still exist in undiminished
vigour when some traveller from New Zealand shall, in the midst of
a vast solitude, take his stand on a broken arch of London Bridge to
sketch the ruins of St Paul's.
On *Leopold von Ranke's* History of the Popes

Karl Marx
Religion is the sigh of the oppressed creature, the feeling of a
heartless world and the soul of soulless circumstances. It is the
opium of the people.
  Critique of the Hegelian Philosophy of Right

The first requisite for the happiness of the people is the abolition of
religion.
  Ibid

William Lamb, 2nd Viscount Melbourne
Things have come to a pretty pass when religion is allowed to invade the sphere of private life.
  Attributed

John Milton
New Presbyter is but old Priest writ large.
  Sonnet: On the New forcers of Conscience under the Long Parliament

  What in me is dark
Illumine, what is low raise and support;
That to the highth of this great argument
I may assert eternal Providence,
And justify the ways of God to men.
  Paradise Lost

Better to reign in hell, than serve in heav'n.
  Ibid

Michel Eyquem de Montaigne
Man cannot make a worm, yet he will make gods by the dozen.
  Essays

Charles Louis de Secondat, Baron de Montesquieu
If triangles had a god, he would have three sides.
  Lettres Persanes

Novalis [Friedrich Leopold von Hardenberg]
Gott-trunkener Mensch.
A God-intoxicated man [Spinoza].

Sir William Osler
Nothing in life is more wonderful than faith—the one great moving force which we can neither weigh in the balance nor test in the crucible.
  British Medical Journal, 1910

Ovid [Publius Ovidius Naso]
There is a god within us, and we glow when he stirs us.
  Fasti

Thomas Paine
Every religion is good that teaches man to be good.
  The Rights of Man

Blaise Pascal
Men never do evil so completely and cheerfully as when they do it from religious conviction.
  Pensées

William Pitt the Elder
We have a Calvinistic creed, a Popish liturgy, and an Arminian clergy.
  House of Lords speech, 1770

Alexander Pope
  Some to church repair
Not for the doctrine, but the music there.
  Essay on Criticism

Laugh where we must, be candid where we can;
But vindicate the ways of God to man.
  An Essay on Man

An honest Man's the noblest work of God.
  Ibid

Ernest Renan
O Lord, if there is a Lord, save my soul, if I have a soul.
  Prière d'un Sceptique

Arthur Schopenhauer
Faith is like love: it cannot be forced.
  Parerga und Paralipomena

William Shakespeare
He wears his faith but as the fashion of his hat.
  Much Ado About Nothing 1

There are no tricks in plain and simple faith.
  Julius Caesar 4

There are more things in heaven and earth, Horatio,
Than are dreamt of in your philosophy.
Hamlet 1

Our remedies oft in ourselves do lie,
Which we ascribe to heaven.
All's Well That Ends Well 1

As flies to wanton boys, are we to gods;
They kill us for their sport.
King Lear 4

Heaven is above all yet; there sits a judge
That no king can corrupt.
King Henry VIII 3

George Bernard Shaw
There is only one religion, though there are a hundred versions of it.
Plays Unpleasant, Preface

In heaven an angel is nobody in particular.
Man and Superman: Maxims for Revolutionists

Must then a Christ perish in torment in every age to save those that
have no imagination?
St Joan

Percy Bysshe Shelley
Earth groans beneath religion's iron age
And priests dare babble of a God of peace
Even whilst their hands are red with guiltless blood.
Queen Mab

Hell is a city much like London—
   A populous and a smoky city.
Peter Bell the Third

Sydney Smith
As the French say, there are three sexes—men, women, and
clergymen.
   Lady Holland's *Memoir of the Rev. Sydney Smith*

Jonathan Swift
We have just enough religion to make us hate, but not enough to
make us love one another.
   Thoughts on Various Subjects; from Miscellanies

Thomas Szasz
If you talk to God, you are praying, if God talks to you, you have
schizophrenia. If the dead talk to you, you are a spiritualist, if God
talks to you, you are a schizophrenic.
   The Second Sin

Alfred, Lord Tennyson
Kind hearts are more than coronets,
   And simple faith than Norman blood.
   Lady Clara Vere de Vere

There lives more faith in honest doubt,
Believe me, than in half the creeds.
   In Memoriam

One God, one law, one element,
   And one far-off divine event,
To which the whole creation moves.
   Ibid

More things are wrought by prayer
Than this world dreams of.
   Idylls of the King: The Passing of Arthur

William Makepeace Thackeray
'Tis not the dying for a faith that's so hard, Master Harry—every man
of every nation has done that—'tis the living up to it that is difficult.
   The History of Henry Esmond

Virgil [Publius Vergilius Maro]
The will of the gods was otherwise.
   Aeneid

Rudolf Virchow
There can be no scientific dispute with respect to faith, for science

and faith exclude one another.
Disease, Life, and Man

Voltaire [François Marie Arouet]
Si Dieu n'existait pas, il faudrait l'inventer.
If God did not exist, it would be necessary to invent him.

Epitre à l'auteur du nouveau livre des trois imposteurs.
God is always on the side of the heaviest battalions.
Letter, 1770

Oscar (Fingall O'Flahertie Wills) Wilde
Religions die when they are proved to be true. Science is the record of dead religions.
Phrases and Philosophies: for the Use of the Young: Chameleon

(Adeline) Virginia Woolf
I read the book of Job last night—I don't think God comes well out of it.
Letter to Lytton Strachey

William Wordsworth
But trailing clouds of glory do we come
 From God, who is our home:
Heaven lies about us in our infancy!
Ode on Intimations of Immortality

Thomas Russell Ybarra
A Christian is a man who feels
Repentance on a Sunday
For what he did on Saturday
And is going to do on Monday.
The Christian

Edward Young
A God all mercy, is a God unjust
Night Thoughts

Mankind

Aristotle
The high-minded man does not bear grudges, for it is not the mark of a great soul to remember injuries, but to forget them.
The Nicomachean Ethics

At his best man is the noblest of all animals; separated from law and justice, he is the worst.
Politics

Man is by nature a political animal.
Ibid

Neil (Alden) Armstrong
That's one small step for a man, one giant leap for mankind.
Stepping on to the moon's surface, 21 July 1969

Phineas Taylor Barnum
There's a sucker born every minute.
Attributed

Simone de Beauvoir
It is not in giving but in risking life that man is raised above the animal; that is why superiority has been accorded in humanity not to the sex that brings forth but to that which kills.
The Second Sex

Carl Lotus Becker
[Man] alone can stand apart imaginatively and, regarding himself and the universe in their eternal aspects, pronounce a judgment: the significance of man is that he is insignificant and is aware of it.
Progress and Power

Ambrose (Gwinett) Bierce
Man: An animal so lost in rapturous contemplation of what he thinks

he is as to overlook what he indubitably ought to be.
The Devil's Dictionary

Karen Blixen [Isak Dinesen]
What is man, when you come to think upon him, but a minutely set, ingenious machine for turning, with infinite artfulness, the red wine of Shiraz into urine?
Seven Gothic Tales, 'The Dreamers'

Robert Browning
Love, hope, fear, faith—these make humanity;
These are its sign and note and character.
Paracelsus

Robert Burns
Man's inhumanity to man.
Man Was Made to Mourn

Confucius
The nature of men is always the same; it is their habits that separate them.
Analects

Ralph Waldo Emerson
No law can be sacred to me but that of my nature. Good and bad are but names very readily transferable to that or this; the only right is what is after my own constitution; the only wrong what is against it.
Essays: Self-Reliance

Clifton Fadiman
Experience teaches you that this man who looks you straight in the eye, particularly if he adds a firm handshake, is hiding something.
Enter, Conversing

Anne Frank
In spite of eveything I still believe that people are really good at heart.
The Diary of a Young Girl

Sir W(illiam) S(chwenck) Gilbert
Man is Nature's sole mistake.
Princess Ida

(Henry) Graham Greene
In human relations kindness and lies are worth a thousand truths.
   The Heart of the Matter

Ernest Hemingway
I know only that what is moral is what you feel good after and what
is immoral is what you feel bad after.
   Death in the Afternoon

Homer
Of all the creatures that creep and breathe on the earth there is none
more wretched than man.
   Iliad

Aldous (Leonard) Huxley
That all men are equal is a proposition to which, at ordinary times,
no sane individual has ever given his assent.
   Proper Studies

Rudyard Kipling
Horrible, hairy, human.
   The Truce of the Bear

Charles Lamb
The human species, according to the best theory I can form of it, is
composed of two distinct races, the men who borrow, and the men
who lend.
   Essays of Elia: The Two Races of Men

François, Duc de La Rochefoucauld
Nothing is rarer than true good nature; they who are reputed to have
it are generally only pliant and weak.
   Maxims

Marcus Aurelius
Let us put an end, once for all, to this discussion of what a good man
should be—and be one.
   Meditations

W(illiam) Somerset Maugham

I'll give you my opinion of the human race...Their heart's in the right place, but their head is a thoroughly inefficient organ.

The Summing Up

Charles Louis de Secondat, Baron de Montesquieu

The lower animals have not the high advantages that we have, but they have something that we lack. They know nothing of our hopes, but they also know nothing of our fears; they are subject to death as we are, but they are not aware of it.

The Spirit of the Laws

George Augustus Moore

Humanity is a pigsty where liars, hypocrites and the obscene in spirit congregate.

Confessions of a Young Man

Octavio Paz

Solitude lies at the lowest depth of the human condition. Man is the only being who feels himself to be alone and the only one who is searching for the Other.

The Labyrinth of Solitude

Plato

Man is a tame, a domesticated animal.

Laws

Pliny the Elder

Man is the only animal that knows nothing, and can learn nothing without being taught. He can neither speak nor walk nor eat, nor do anything at the prompting of nature, but only weep.

Natural History

Alexander Pope

Hope springs eternal in the human breast:
Man never is, but always to be blest.

An Essay on Man

Francis Quarles
Man is Heaven's masterpiece.
  Emblems, Bk 2

Sir Walter Alexander Raleigh
I wish I loved the Human Race;
I wish I loved its silly face;
I wish I liked the way it walks;
I wish I liked the way it talks;
And when I'm introduced to one
I wish I thought What Jolly Fun!
  Laughter from a Cloud

Antoine de Saint-Exupéry
It is only with the heart that one can see rightly; what is essential is invisible to the eye.
  The Little Prince

George Santayana
The mass of mankind is divided into two classes, the Sancho Panzas who have a sense for reality, but no ideals, and the Don Quixotes with a sense for ideals, but mad.
  Interpretations of Poetry and Religion, Preface

Franz (Peter) Schubert
Let us take men as they are, not as they ought to be.
  Diary, 16 June 1816

Charles Monroe Schulz
I love mankind, it's people I can't stand.
  Go Fly a Kite, Charlie Brown

Seneca
Man is a social animal.
  De Beneficiis

Man is a reasoning animal.
  Epistolæ ad Lucilium

William Shakespeare

Love all, trust a few,
Do wrong to none: be able for thine enemy
Rather in power than use, and keep thy friend
Under thy own life's key: be check'd for silence,
But never tax'd for speech.

All's Well That Ends Well 1

Richard Brinsley Sheridan

Certainly nothing is unnatural that is not physically impossible.

The Critic

Robert Southey

Man is a dupable animal. Quacks in medicine, quacks in religion,
and quacks in politics know this, and act upon that knowledge.

The Doctor

Terence [Publius Terentius Afer]

Homo sum; humani nihil a me alienum puto.
I am a man; and nothing human is foreign to me.

Heauton Timoroumenos

Henry David Thoreau

The mass of men lead lives of quiet desperation. What is called
resignation is confirmed desperation.

Walden

Mark Twain [Samuel Langhorne Clemens]

The noblest work of God? Man. Who found it out? Man.

Autobiography

Man is the only animal that blushes. Or needs to.

Following the Equator

The fact that man knows right from wrong proves his intellectual
superiority to the other creatures; but the fact that he can do wrong
proves his moral inferiority to any creature that cannot.

What is Man?

Sir Jan Laurens Van der Post
Human beings are perhaps never more frightening than when they are convinced beyond doubt that they are right.
The Lost World of the Kalahari

Marquis de Luc de Clapiers Vauvenargues
We should expect the best and the worst from mankind, as from the weather.
Reflections and Maxims

Voltaire [François Marie Arouet]
Animals have these advantages over man: they never hear the clock strike, they die without any idea of death, they have no theologians to instruct them, their last moments are not disturbed by unwelcome and unpleasant ceremonies, their funerals cost them nothing, and no one starts lawsuits over their wills.
Letter, 1769

William Wordsworth
The still, sad music of humanity
Tintern Abbey

Life

Hans Christian Andersen
Every man's life is a fairy-tale written by God's fingers.
Works, Preface

P(hilip) J(ames) Bailey
It matters not how long we live, but how.
Festus: Wood and Water

The Bible
For what is your life? It is even a vapour, that appeareth for a little time, and then vanisheth away.
James 4

Samuel Butler
Is life worth lliving? This is a question for an embryo, not for a man.

To live is like love, all reason is against it, and all healthy instinct for it.
Notebooks

Nicolas Chamfort
Living is a sickness from which sleep provides relief every sixteen hours. It's a pallative. The remedy is death.

Abraham Cowley
Life is an incurable Disease.
Pindarique Odes

George Crabbe
Life is not measured by the time we live.
The Village

Dinah Maria Mulock Craik
The secret of life is not to do what one likes, but to try to like that which one has to do.

Emily Dickinson

I took one draught of life,
I'll tell you what I paid,
Precisely an existence—
The market-price, they said.
  Further Poems

Guy Carleton Drewry

Ah, life could be so beautiful, Yet never is.
  Father and Son

Ralph Waldo Emerson

Life is good only when it is magical and musical, a perfect timing
and consent, and when we do not anatomize it.
  Society and Solitude: Works and Days

Life is a festival only to the wise. Seen from the nook and chimney-
side of prudence, it wears a ragged and dangerous front.
  Essays, First Series: Heroism

Donald Evans

Born with a monocle he stares at life,
And sends his soul on pensive promenades.
  En Monocle

Sir William Schwenck Gilbert

Life's a pudding full of plums,
Care's a canker that benumbs,
  Wherefore waste our elocution
  On impossible solution?
  Life's a pleasant institution,
Let us take it as it comes!
  The Gondoliers 1

Thomas Hardy

For life I've never cared greatly,
As worth a man's while.
  For Life I Had Never Cared Greatly

William Hazlitt
The most rational cure after all for the inordinate fear of death is to set a just value on life.
Table Talk

Katharine Hepburn
Life's what's important. Walking, houses, family. Birth and pain and joy.

Thomas Hobbes
The life of man, solitary, poor, nasty, brutish, and short.
Leviathan: Of Man

Elbert Hubbard
Life is simply one damn thing after another.
Attributed

Dr Samuel Johnson
Life must be filled up, and the man who is not capable of intellectual pleasures must content himself with such as his senses can afford.
Mrs Piozzi's *Johnsoniana*

That kind of life is most happy which affords us the most opportunities of gaining our own esteem.
Works

Harriet Eleanor King
Measure thy life by loss instead of gain;
Not by the wine drunk, but by the wine poured forth.
The Disciples

Fran Lebowitz
Life is something to do when you can't get to sleep.
The Observer, 21 Jan. 1979

Jean de La Bruyère
There are only three events in a man's life; birth, life, and death; he is not conscious of being born, he dies in pain, and he forgets to live.
Caracteres

Edgar Lee Masters
It takes life to love Life.
  Lucinda Matlock

Herman Melville
Life's a voyage that's homeward bound.
  Cournos' *Modern Plutarch*

H(enry) L(ouis) Mencken
The basic fact about human existence is not that it is a tragedy, but that it is a bore.
  Prejudices

Edna St Vincent Millay
It is not true that life is one damn thing after another—it's one damn thing over and over.
  Letters of Edna St Vincent Millay

Wilson Mizner
Life's a tough proposition, and the first hundred years are the hardest.

Michel Eyquem de Montaigne
Mon métier et mon art, c'est vivre.
My business and my art is to live.
  Essays

Were I to live my life over again, I should live it just as I have done. I neither complain of the past, nor fear the future.
  Ibid

Ovid [Publius Ovidius Naso]
Vive pius; moriere pius.
Live righteously; you shall die righteously.
  Amores

Stephen Phillips
How good it is to live, even at the worst!
  Christ in Hades

Arthur Schopenhauer

Each day is a little life; every walking and rising a little birth, every fresh morning a little youth, every going to rest and sleep a little death.

Our Relation to Ourselves

Seneca

Quemadmodum vivas, quamdiu vivas.
As long as you live, keep learning how to live.

Epistulæ ad Lucilium

Cotidie cum vita paria faciamus.
Let us balance life's account avery day.

Ibid

William Shakespeare

All the world's a stage,
And all the men and women merely players:
They have their exits and their entrances;
And one man in his time plays many parts,
Its acts being seven ages.

As You Like It 2

Life's but a walking shadow, a poor player
That struts and frets his hour upon the stage,
And then is heard no more; it is a tale
Told by an idiot, full of sound and fury
Signifying nothing.

Macbeth 5

Life is as tedious as a twice-told tale,
Vexing the dull ear of a drowsy man.

King John 3

George Bernard Shaw

Life is a disease; and the only difference between one man and another is the stage of the disease at which he lives.

Back to Methuselah

LIFE

There are two tragedies in life. One is not to get your heart's desire. The other is to get it.

Man and Superman

(Lloyd) Logan Pearsall Smith
There are two things to aim at in life: first, to get what you want; and, after that, to enjoy it. Only the wisest of mankind achieve the second.

Afterthoughts

Henry David Thoreau
I love a life whose plot is simple,
And does not thicken with every pimple.

Conscience

Virgil [Publius Vergilius Maro]
Pone aurem vellens, "vivite," ait, "venio"
Set forth the wine and the dice, and perish who thinks of
tomorrow!
Here's Death twitching my ear, "Live," says he, "for I'm
coming!"

Copa

Israel Zangwill
Oh, for the simple life,
For tents and starry skies!

Aspirations

Author Index

A

Acheson, Dean *(1893–1971)* 130

Acton, Lord *(1834–1902)* 48, 188

Adams, Franklin P. *(1881–1960)* 19

Adams, Henry *(1838–1918)* 12, 102, 177

Adams, John Quincy *(1767–1848)* 42

Addison, Joseph *(1672–1719)* 33, 113, 145, 182, 198

Aeschylus *(525–456 BC)* 36

Albery, James *(1838–89)* 136

Alcott, Bronson *(1799–1888)* 87, 156, 182

Alexander the Great *(356–323 BC)* 33

Alfonso the Wise *(1221–84)* 56

Allen, Fred *(1894–1956)* 48

Allen, Woody *(1935–)* 22, 48, 76, 212

Ames, Fisher *(1758–1808)* 192

Amiel, Henri Frédéric *(1821–81)* 12, 48

Amis, Kingsley*(1922–)* 22, 120

Anacreon *(c.500–428 BC)* 52, 91

Anaxandrides *(fl. 376 BC)* 22

Andersen, Hans Christian *(1805–75)* 236

Anderson, Maxwell *(1888–1941)* 76

Andrewes, Lancelot *(1555–1626)* 217

Anouilh, Jean *(1910–87)* 166

Anthony, Susan B. *(1820–1906)* 81, 192

Antiphanes of Macedonia *(fl. 360 BC)* 177

Aristophanes *(c.448–c.388 BC)* 12, 81, 188

Aristotle *(384–322 BC)* 42, 102, 141, 192, 229

Armistead, Lewis *(1817–63)* 108

Armstrong, Neil *(1930–)* 229

Arnold, Matthew *(1822–88)* 151

Attlee, Clement *(1883–1967)* 192

Auden, W. H. *(1907–73)* 166

Augustine, St *(354–430)* 56, 76, 198, 217

Austen, Jane *(1775–1817)* 7, 36, 65, 81, 87, 145, 156

B

Bach, Alvan L. 126

Bacon, Francis *(1561–1626)* 22, 42, 48, 52, 59, 81, 87, 95, 98, 102, 113, 156, 182, 188, 205, 208, 212

Bagehot, Walter *(1826–77)* 42, 56, 177, 217

Bailey, P. J. *(1816–1902)* 236

C

E

I

J

K

W

Y

Z